Grace Upon Grace

Sacramental Theology and the Christian Life

Second Edition

Gregory S. Neal

WESTBOW·
PRESS
A DIVISION OF THOMAS NELSON
& ZONDERVAN

First Edition, 2000
Second Edition, 2014

WestBow Press books may be ordered through booksellers or by contacting:

WestBow Press
A Division of Thomas Nelson & Zondervan
1663 Liberty Drive
Bloomington, IN 47403
www.westbowpress.com
1 (866) 928-1240

ISBN: 978-1-4908-6006-0 (sc)
ISBN: 978-1-4908-6008-4 (hc)
ISBN: 978-1-4908-6007-7 (e)

Library of Congress Control Number: 2014920756

Printed in the United States of America.

WestBow Press rev. date: 12/19/2014

Dedication

In memory of my Father:
Charles Mayo Neal, Sr.

And

In honor of my Mother:
Lona Mae Neal

"From his fullness we have all received, grace upon grace."
—John 1:16

Contents

Foreword

By Bishop William B Oden

I am pleased to invite you to read Gregory Neal's *Grace Upon Grace*. This tightly written volume lays a strong foundation for a Wesleyan Theology using Grace as the integrative theme. The author has a terse readable style and the contents are most informative.

The book stays close to Wesley's own thought and will be a godsend to pastors, Sunday school teachers, and interested laypersons. In a time of resurgence of Wesleyan Theology, this volume makes a significant contribution.

Neal's emphasis on the "sacramental" is especially refreshing. Wesleyan denominations are in the midst of sacramental re-centering and the author is helpful in defining and imaging our Eucharistic and baptismal theology. He also expands on other sacramental acts.

I heartily recommend this book.

> Dr. William B. Oden
> Bishop of the Dallas Episcopal Area,
> The United Methodist Church
> 1996 – 2004

Preface

This book has been written for *you*. It matters not if you are laity or clergy, Arminian or Calvinist, Protestant or Catholic; it matters not if you have an extensive background in theology or just a burning desire to find out more about the grace of Jesus Christ—if you've picked up this book, it's for *you*. This is not a work of "high-powered" academic scholarship, nor is it intended to be devotional reading, though one may find a bit of both here. Rather, in these pages I have attempted to translate the strange, often confusing complexity of academic scholarship into terms and expressions, stories and concepts that those in the pulpit and those in the pew can understand and apply in their everyday Christian lives. If I have succeeded in this endeavor, then this book will have achieved its purpose.

This is the second edition of this book. It has been substantially revised and expanded with an eye toward conveying more information with greater clarity and in a more fluid style. While most of my conclusions have remained unchanged, over the past decade-and-a-half I have developed greater precision and maturity in my theological and spiritual perspectives. Additionally, the first edition was published during a very difficult period of my life and ministry; some of this was quite apparent within its pages, coloring both my opinions and approach. I have attempted to better reflect the result of God's work in my life in this second edition.

Apart from the first edition, certain elements of this book have appeared elsewhere in a substantially different format. Segments of several chapters may be discerned within some of the articles and academic papers published on my website (www.RevNeal.org). While much of my poetry, contained herein, has also been published before, these verses have remained my property.

I would like to express my warmest regards to my friends and fellow clergy in several denominations, a few of whom have recently gone on to join the great cloud of witnesses in the Communion of the Saints: the Rev. Gene Gordon, the Rev. Kathleen Baskin-Ball, Dr. Thomas Waitschies, Dr. Leta Gorham, Dr. Gary Butner, the Rev. Jeff Garrett, and Fr. Benedict Ashley. Their many constructive remarks on numerous aspects of the text during the formation of either the first or second editions were invaluable.

From Duke Divinity School, Dr. Thomas A. Langford gave much time and attention to a preliminary version of the first edition. Even though his life was near its end, this brilliant theologian took enough interest in a former student to offer remarks, guidance, and words of support in review of my work. Thank you, Dr. Langford, for being a faithful teacher to the end. Similarly, Dr. Gayle Carlton Felton kindly reviewed the first edition and made many helpful suggestions when I began revising the text for this second edition; her guidance and words of encouragement were golden. I only regret that she didn't live to see it completed.

Dr. William B. Oden, past President of the Council of Bishops and retired Bishop of the North Texas Conference of The United Methodist Church, was very kind to read through the original manuscript and offered many gracious comments for the first edition. Some of his suggestions regarding the importance of ecumenical concerns have been taken to heart in the second edition. Thank you, Bishop Oden, for your valuable time!

I want to thank my good friends, Mr. Christopher Milligan, Mrs. Gail Blythe, and Ms. Carolyn Trezevant, each of whom devoted many hours to reading and editing the entire manuscript. Their numerous comments and questions regarding the content of the book, and their many editorial adjustments to its grammar irregularities, were critical to the final stages of the second edition.

The Monks of the Anglican Society of Saint John the Evangelist deserve a special note. I would like to thank the late Br. Paul Wessinger, whose spiritual direction made all the difference to me in my decision to continue in ministry in The United Methodist Church, and whose prayers and wise spiritual counsel saw me through many tough valleys in life and ministry. I would also like to offer my love and sincere regards to Brothers Eldridge, Brian, David, Curtis, Jonathan, Martin, and to Bishop Tom Shaw, as well as the late Brothers Carl, Adam, Bob, and especially Fr. Gross, for their love and support, their prayers and concern. I have always found a safe, quiet, welcoming home among these men of God, and I praise Jesus that this monastic community has continued to be a source of support for me in my ministry.

Dr. Gregory S. Neal
Dallas, Texas
Sixth Sunday After Pentecost, 2014

O Thou who this mysterious bread
Didst in Emmaus break,
Return herewith our souls to feed,
and to thy followers speak.

Unseal the volume of thy grace
Apply the gospel word;
Open our eyes to see thy face
Our hearts to know the Lord.

Of thee communing still
We mourn till thou the veil remove;
Talk with us, and our hearts shall burn
With flames of fervent love.

Enkindle now the heavenly zeal,
And make thy mercy known,
And give our pardoned souls to feel
That God and love are one.

Charles Wesley, 1745
UM Hymnal #613

Chapter One

The Means of Grace

When I was a child I always looked forward to the arrival of the ice cream truck. The instant I heard that distinctive music playing in the distance I would go running into the house to beg my mom for some money. I would bounce up and down with excitement, impatiently waiting while mother dug in her purse for a dollar. Then, money in hand, I would run back outside to wait at the curb, with great expectation, as that truck slowly inched its way toward our house. It never came fast enough. It always seemed as though there were a billion other children between that truck and me I can distinctly remember being afraid that it would run out of ice cream by the time it got to my end of the block. But arrive it finally did, and by that time my imagination had already eaten its way through half of their stock, and I knew precisely what I wanted.

"The Chocolate Bomb!"

Ah, the joys of childhood! The joys of the simple, uncomplicated pleasures that come with ice cream bars and the heat of the summer months. The innocent expectation and excitement that filled those days! Today, right this very instant, there's a half gallon of chocolate ice cream in the freezer in my kitchen—ice cream that I bought with my own money, and from which I can dip several heaping scoops any time I want. But it's just not the same.

The ice cream that came from the truck was *special*. Those bars were not like the ice cream in my freezer; the ice cream in my freezer is mine, thanks to the effort of my labors—I earned the money with which I bought today's ice cream. I went to the grocery store and selected it from all the other choices. I checked its label for fat content (oh, the *horrible* things we do to ice cream these days!), and I looked around to see if they had any of the other special flavors that I like (coffee ice cream … yum, yum). Then I bought the ice cream, paying for it with my own money.

I *earned* that ice cream with a sermon, a Bible study, and several pastoral visits; I earned the joy in my mouth and my stomach that the ice cream would bring with service and work! But it's still not the same as those simple chocolate bars that came from the ice cream truck during my childhood. You see, *those* ice cream bars were unexpected, wonderful gifts that appeared in the heat of the afternoon to excite and refresh a young child's spirit. I didn't have to work hard to get those ice cream bars. If my allowance had already been spent for the week, I could always count on Mother to fork over enough for me to buy an ice cream anyway. No, those ice creams of my childhood days were wonderful and free; and so much unlike the ice cream of today, because I didn't do anything to earn them. They were an undeserved gift—and a wonderful one at that! Essentially, they were grace incarnate.

Which brings us to the topic of this book: what is grace and how is it received?

We've all heard the common expression: *She walked with much grace.* When the word *grace* is used in this way, it generally conveys a sense of "refinement" and "gentility," often as an attitudinal quality that has been developed through education and training. However, if we're speaking theologically, *grace* is a specific and essential, yet very simple, thing; in Greek, the language of the New Testament, *grace* is the word:

$$\chi\alpha\rho\iota\varsigma$$

Pronounced "kharis," this word literally means "unmerited favor."[1] For something to be "grace," it must be unearned, undeserved, freely given, and freely received. If it is "grace," it cannot be earned or made; no work of your own can go into producing it.

Divine grace is essential for Christian living. It is so essential that, without it, we lack the ability even to turn to God or have faith in Jesus Christ. Human beings have fallen so far away from God's will, through self-centered sin and self-righteousness, that we are fundamentally incapable of even wanting to know God, much less being able to actually say yes to God's love. Thanks to what is known in Augustinian theology as "the fall," all human beings are without hope and are entirely incapable of seeking after God unless God is *first* acting upon our hearts. Apart from the grace of God, we are utterly lost. This "lostness" calls for God's initiative, God's power, and God's transforming presence. And all of this—the desire to know God, the ability to say yes to God, and the act of faith involved in actually saying yes—comes to us through grace. Indeed, each stage of the Christian life, each step that we take toward God, is entirely the product of God's loving, empowering grace, which draws, enables, transforms, and empowers us.

Since grace is central to the Christian life, questions automatically arise: how does one receive it? What does grace look like? How does grace function? And by what *means* does grace come to us? These kinds of questions are part of the field of systematic theology known as sacramentology, the subject that occupies a substantial portion of this book.

By what means does one receive grace?

I receive phone calls by means of a telephone. I watch the news by means of a television. I make cash withdrawals from my bank account by means of an Automatic Teller Machine. I read e-mails by means of my computer. Each of these devices is a means through which I

---

[1]   Walter Bauer, ed., *A Greek-English Lexicon of the New Testament and Other Early Christian Literature* (Chicago: University of Chicago Press, 1979), 877–878.

receive something. Likewise, when we talk about the means of grace we're referencing the ways, methods, and instruments through which God's grace comes to us.

Human beings are creatures of instrumentality; many different kinds of instruments are a part of our daily experience. Thanks to our experience and our nature as beings with physical limitations, it makes perfect sense for us to think about doing things and receiving information through instruments. Be it by means of a TV, radio, or telephone, an ATM or a computer, we usually conceive of receiving items or information by way of a device. In Christian theology, the means of grace function as the methods, the ways, the instruments through which God makes divine grace available to us and for us.

This is the essence of the sacramental approach to the role and function of grace in the Christian life. It is the approach of the Roman Catholic, Eastern Orthodox, Anglican, Lutheran, Methodist, and Presbyterian churches, as well as those faith communities that are theologically related to them in their doctrinal perspective on the means of grace. In other words, the largest portion of historic Christianity accepts the sacramental approach to the function and receipt of grace. Throughout the course of this book, when I reference these communities I will use the terms *sacramental* and *catholic*. Elsewhere, I tend to use the term catholic (with a lowercase *c*) in its sense of "universal," meaning all Christians; but relative to the issue of one's understanding of the functioning of grace, I will be using it in this confined sense.

Those churches which come from the separatist wing of the Protestant Reformation—particularly Baptist, Church of Christ, the so-called "non-denominational" and "Bible" churches, and any others who are theologically related to them—generally do not share this approach to the means of grace. Rather than believing that grace comes to believers through instruments, they understand the means of grace as being good works that Christians perform in obedience to the commandment of Christ. If God's grace is actually present to believers in any way relative to these works, it is only present *directly* from God and not through any instrumentality.

This approach is known as ordinance theology, and it tends to deny that there is any kind of actual, instrumental presence in these ordinances. We do them, according to this approach, out of obedience to the Lord's commandment. Throughout the course of this book, when I reference this group I will generally use the terms *ordinance, reformed, non-sacramental,* and *Zwinglian.*[2]

While sacramental theology theoretically makes room for grace to be received through non-instrumental means, proposed examples of this are exceedingly rare. Indeed, when examples have been offered it has been my invariable experience that one or more instruments can be identified, functioning somewhere in the process. Fundamentally, the two approaches are incompatible with each other; they reflect two contradictory conceptions of how grace functions and how we receive it.

There are many means of grace. Throughout the history of the church Christians have identified and institutionalized several of them as either sacraments or sacramental acts, and each has played an important role in the lives of believers. Other means of grace have been recognized as having sacramental qualities but only infrequently have they been recognized among the sacraments. While there are far too many for us to examine within the confines of this book, we will look at a few of the more important means of grace, study how they function, and consider how their sacramental qualities play a role in the life and witness of Christians.

---

[2]   The role and nature of the ordinances in Zwinglian theology will be covered in chapter three.

Questions for Reflection and Discussion

Chapter One

♦ What does grace mean to you?

♦ How do you understand the term *means of grace?*

♦ Do you believe that grace can come to you directly, apart from any specific means? If so, describe an example of such.

♦ If you believe that God's grace comes to us through instrumental means, list those which have a special significance for you.

♦ Consider those things or people who have been special means of grace for you. What have they said or done to express the love of God in your life?

♦ How are you expressing the grace of God to others? Are there any ways that you could become a more effective means of grace for those around you?

♦ Do you believe it is possible to live a Christian life divorced from all of the means of grace?

In Brilliant Rays of Grace

Through the darkness of the night,
    The gloomy death of sin,
Shines the brilliant spark of light,
    Of grace and peace within.

Jesus comes now unto us,
    In brilliant rays of grace,
And though we be as dead as dust,
    His grace will shine upon our face.

His grace enlightens our dead hearts,
    His peace does calm our souls,
His loving presence never parts,
    And we are held within the fold.

Give to Jesus now your life,
    Open your eyes unto His light,
Let Him lift your downcast sight,
    And change you by His might.

Gregory S. Neal †
January 1996

Chapter Two

The Stages of Grace

T he founder of the Methodist revival in the Church of England, and of the Methodist Episcopal Church in the United States, was an Anglican priest named John Wesley. Wesley was an especially gifted theologian and preacher, one of several from a family of well-respected clerics. His father, Samuel Wesley, was a noted pastor, scholar, and poet, while his mother and chief educator, Susanna, was the exceedingly literate and devout daughter of the Puritan scholar, Dr. Samuel Annesley. John's brother, Charles, was not only the co-founder of the Methodist revival in the Church of England but also has been considered one of the greatest hymn writers of the eighteenth century English Church.[3]

To tell the story of John Wesley's life and ministry would require several books.[4] Suffice it to say that John Wesley served, for a short period of time, as both a missionary pastor in Savannah, Georgia, and as an instructor at Oxford University; but he is best known as the irrepressible open-air evangelist and Anglican reformer who claimed the world as his parish.[5]

John Wesley had a deep and abiding interest in applying systematic theology—what he termed "practical divinity"—to everyday Christian living.[6] He tended to shun purely theoretical arguments,

---

[3] Frederick Norwood, *The Story of American Methodism* (Nashville: Abingdon Press, 1974), 23–25.
[4] For more on the life of John Wesley, see especially Richard P. Heitzenrater, *The Illusive Mr. Wesley* Vols. 1 and 2 (Nashville: Abingdon Press, 1987). See also, by the same author, *Wesley and the People called Methodists* (Nashville: Abingdon Press, 1994).
[5] Norwood, 26–41.
[6] Thomas Langford, *Practical Divinity: Theology in the Wesleyan Tradition* (Nashville: Abingdon Press, 1983), 5.

preferring theological approaches which made sense of the Christian experience. Throughout his long life John was an eclectic synthesizer of theology and tradition; in his formative years as a pastor and theologian, he was not afraid to draw from a broad range of both historic and contemporary Christian sources as he formulated his theology and established his religious practices. In this sense, as in many others, he was both very Anglican and also a man ahead of his time. Early in his ministry John Wesley became an Arminian, applying many significant elements of this broad theological system to his personal theology and, subsequently, to the life and faith of his Methodist societies.

Arminianism is a moderate theological revision of Calvinism that limits the significance of predestination to divine foreknowledge. It takes its name from its founder, Jacobus Arminius (1560–1609), who was a Dutch Reformed pastor and theologian. In 1603, when Arminius became professor of theology at the University of Leiden, he found himself defending his position that God's sovereignty and human free will are, at least functionally, fully compatible. The conflict between the Arminian approach and that of the Calvinists would become legendary, with violence and heresy trials and all the usual trappings of religious intolerance. Indeed, the debate is still not over: just a cursory look at the multitude of internet websites which focus on the subject demonstrates that Calvinists and Arminians often find it difficult to live together in peace. [7]

John Wesley adopted Arminianism, best reflecting his own theological approach; indeed, he so identified with the movement that in 1778 he began publication of *The Arminian* magazine.[8] Fundamental to Arminian theology is a rejection of several of the central precepts of Calvinism and an emphasis on the universal application of divine grace. Arminius believed that Jesus died for the sins of all humanity, and that hence God's grace is understood as being available to all

---

[7]   For more on the life and ministry of Jacobus Arminius see Carl Bangs, *Arminius: A Study in the Dutch Reformation* (Grand Rapids: Asbury Press, 1985).

[8]   Norwood, 26–41.

regardless of response. Contrary to this position, Calvinism teaches that God has predestined certain people—the "elect"—to salvation, that Jesus died only for the elect, that only after their salvation are these elected individuals regenerated, and that it is impossible for the elect to lose their salvation. In this approach, God's grace is not available to all because Jesus died only for the sins of the elect.[9]

Calvinism can be easily outlined through the use of the classic acronym *TULIP,* in which each letter stands for a different precept of the Calvinist doctrine:

T= ***Total Depravity.*** All human beings are entirely devoid of any spark of divine light. We are totally dead and are entirely incapable of doing God's will or even of just wanting to come to Jesus.

U= ***Unconditional Election.*** Those whom God wishes to save are saved not by anything that God sees or knows about the individual in question, but rather entirely due to God's will. Some are unconditionally elected to salvation, and some are not (this is known as "Supralapsarianism," or what I frequently like to call "double-barreled predestination"). In all fairness, John Calvin never stressed the dark side of this doctrine; rather he focused on God's unconditional selection of the Elect.

L= ***Limited Atonement.*** Jesus died for the sins of the Elect, not for the sins of the whole world. Calvinists *must* deny an unlimited atonement because, if not, their next point would make salvation universal.

I= ***Irresistible Grace.*** The grace of Jesus Christ cannot be resisted. Those whom God has elected, and for whom Christ has died, have *no* choice in the matter of salvation—they *must* receive

---

9   Alister E. McGrath, *Christian Theology: An Introduction* (Cambridge: Blackwell Publishing, 1994), 451–454.

God's grace; even if they don't want it, they have no way of saying "no." Essentially, grace becomes a gift that has a mandatory acceptance clause attached.

P= ***Perseverance of the Saints.*** Those whom God has elected, and for whom Christ has died, and to whom God has given divine grace, arc not at any liberty to reject Christ, nor can they in any way lose their salvation.[10]

The doctrines articulated in *TULIP* are a direct consequence of the belief that God's will is sovereign and that human responses to divine grace are unnecessary for salvation. This idea ran contrary to all of Wesley's experience, and hence it is not a surprise that he rejected a large portion of the Calvinist doctrine regarding grace and predestination, adopting most of the tenets of Arminianism.

The doctrine of Total Depravity was one area where Wesley differed with some of Arminius' approach. According to Albert Outler, one of the preeminent Wesleyan theologians of the twentieth century:

> Arminius held that man hath a will to turn to God
> before grace prevents him, whereas for Wesley it is
> the spirit's prevenient motion by which 'we ever are
> moved and inspired to any good thing.'[11]

While Arminius affirmed that it was theoretically possible for a fallen, unregenerate sinner to make an initial turn toward God's calling, he nevertheless affirmed that it was impossible for a fallen sinner to do anything further in actual response to God's call apart from grace. Indeed, based upon Wesley's understanding of the function

---

[10]   Charles Hodge, *Systematic Theology.* 3 Vols. (Grand Rapids: Wm. B. Eerdmans Publishing Co., 1989), Vol. 2, 313–376.

[11]   Kenneth J. Collins, *The Scripture Way of Salvation: the Heart of John Wesley's Theology* (Nashville: Abingdon Press, 1997), 42

and work of prevenient grace, it is entirely possible to conceive of God's call *itself* as an expression of prevenient grace. While not to be confused with the inner workings of the Holy Spirit upon the soul of the unregenerate sinner, this "natural form" of prevenient grace—evident in creation and elsewhere—should not be overlooked as an expression of divine favor. As Jacob Arminius himself wrote:

> Free will is unable to begin or to perfect any true and spiritual good, without grace. That I may not be said, like Pelagius, to practice delusion with regard to the word "grace," I mean by it that which is the grace of Christ and which belongs to regeneration. I affirm, therefore, that this grace is simply and absolutely necessary for the illumination of the mind, the due ordering of the affections, and the inclination of the will to that which is good.[12]

Regardless of how one understands Arminius on the subject of the extent and nature of Total Depravity, John Wesley clearly asserted that *all* human beings are spiritually dead and that it is only God's grace which enables Christians to respond with faith.

This realization can be seen throughout Wesley's sermons and, at length and with much eloquence, in Charles Wesley's Hymns. For example:

> Sinners, turn: why will you die?
> God, your Savior, asks you why.
> God, who did your souls retrieve,
> died himself, that you might live.
> Will you let him die in vain?
> Crucify your Lord again?

---

[12]   James Arminius, *The Works of James Arminius* (Grand Rapids: Baker Book House, 1986), vol. 2, "Grace and Free Will", 427.

Why, you ransomed sinners, why
will you slight his grace, and die?[13]

Wesley argued that the initial offer of grace from the cross of Jesus
Christ comes to all people, everywhere, in the form of prevenient
grace. When sinners willfully and arrogantly refuse to turn away
from their sins, Wesley viewed that as an affront to God's grace: "will
you slight his grace, and die?" In response to God's love, humans are
encouraged (but not compelled) to exercise faith in Jesus Christ and
be saved from the threat of eternal death to the hope of eternal life.

The Arminian approach, as modified by John Wesley, is known
in Methodist Systematic Theology as the *Ordo Salutis,* or "Order
of Salvation."[14] A critical element within Wesley's soteriology[15], it
deals with the presence, application, and function of grace as humans
encounter it during the many various points or stages of their existence.
The Wesleyan *Ordo Salutis* affirms that grace, while ultimately
resistible, is nevertheless essential in enabling the Christian's response
to God's offer of a relationship. Christians must respond to this
invitation by exercising faith and thereby process through the order
of salvation from grace's initial prevenience, to its critical function in
justification, and on to its paramount role in sanctification. Without
exception, grace is the essential element present throughout the entire
order of salvation, enabling the progression from one's beginnings
through to the moment of one's glorification.

How grace functions at the various stages in the Christian life
will differ according to where Christians are in their relationship with
God. In other words, what grace does for us and within us depends
entirely upon where *we* are in our faith development. Contrary to how
the terminology is often used, *Prevenient, Justifying,* and *Sanctifying*
Grace are not different kinds of grace. Rather, there is only one grace:

---

13   *The United Methodist Hymnal: Book of United Methodist Worship* (Nashville: United Methodist
      Publishing House, 1989), 346
14   Collins, 185–186, 188.
15   *Soteriology*: the field of systematic theology that deals with the doctrines of salvation.

God's unmerited favor. We are the ones who are different—the ones who change—not the grace of God.

With this in mind, we will proceed to the *Stages of Grace* and examine how they function throughout the Christian life.

Prevenient Grace

"No one can come to me unless drawn by the Father who sent me."
—John 6:44

We are totally incapable of responding to God without God first calling and empowering our faith. This divine initiative in the process of our salvation is known in theological circles as *prevenient grace.* The word *prevenient* means "before-going" or "going ahead of" and, in this context, describes the first instance of the human encounter with the grace of God. Prior to prevenient grace, we not only lack an ability to say yes to God, we even lack the *desire* to come to God. Prevenient grace both creates and impels our desire, our yearning, our longing for God, while at the same time drawing us to faith in Jesus Christ and making it possible for us to actually exercise that faith. Through prevenient grace God comes to us, in the midst of our condition of being lost—of being spiritually dead—to perform an initial work of transformation within us. In this transformation our thoughts and interests, our inner need for God's love and presence, is brought to life. Indeed, prevenient grace enables us to experience the real, abiding presence of God personally—as parent and sibling, as friend and companion, as savior and guide, as maker, master, and King. It is the very nature of divine love that seeks us out, helps us to recognize our need for God, and then offers us access to God's unlimited, unmerited favor.

Prevenient grace can be illustrated through a very simple story about my tabby cat—a Maine Coon named Bishop Tiggert. When I was in graduate school I lived on the third floor of an apartment building in the middle of a large apartment complex. We all thought that it was a safe place to live; there were hardly ever any strangers about, and we rarely had any criminal activity. And, so, it was a shock when, one night in late spring, I came up the steps to the third landing only to find my apartment door standing open.

I had been robbed!

Fear gripped me. I know I should have run down the steps to a friend's apartment and called the police, but I didn't. I wasn't thinking very clearly. Indeed, I was terrified! I wasn't frightened over the loss of a stereo, TV, VCR, or computer. I wasn't frightened over the possibility that I might get hurt if I barged in on the thief. No, I was terrified that my poor, darling kitty was hurt.

I dashed into the apartment, my heart racing in fear, and flipped on the lights as I entered the living room. There was no sign of my cat. "Tiggert!" I called out, my voice full of fear! "Tiggert! Here, boy!!!!!"

Nothing.

There was no cat anywhere to be seen! Tears streaming down my cheeks, I ran back outside and shouted, *"Tiggert!"* I paused for a moment, then flew down the stairs, checking each floor's landing as I reached it. But, still no cat. I hit the ground floor and dashed out to the front of the building, calling *"Tiggert! Here, boy!"* But, there was no sign of him … anywhere.

By this time I was really crying, afraid that my cat had run away in fear, and was now cowering some place, afraid of the dark and alone in the cold! I rounded the corner of the building, stepping into the deep shadows behind the apartment complex, and immediately saw the long, fluffy tail of my Maine Coon cat, twitching around the corner of the other end of the building!

I dashed toward him, but as I approached his tail vanished around the corner!

"Tiggert!"

I rounded the corner and what I saw stopped me dead in my tracks. There, on the grass, was my tabby Maine Coon, fur up, tail twitching, crouched low and facing off two *big*, mean looking tomcats. I could just see it: Tiggert would leap on one cat and the other one would leap on *him*! Almost immediately, I knew what to do.

I stepped *between* my cat and the two stranger cats, catching their attention as I moved into position. Just then I noticed Tiggert inching forward to crouch between my legs, growling, as I clapped my hands together and shouted, *"get!"*

The two toms *got*. I then leaned over and scooped up my wayward kitty in my arms and carried him to the safety of my apartment and a can of *9 Lives*.

Just as Tiggert got lost, and I searched for him, found him, and scattered the stray cats that night, so also God loves us and comes searching for us wherever we may have wandered. And when God finds us, God scatters the evil "stray cats" of this life, gathers us in, feeds, comforts, and loves us, and takes us home. The God of all creation, the one who fashioned the universe in all of its beauty and awesome majesty, the one who formed us from the primordial elements and breathed into our immortal souls, does this for us.

And this is what prevenient grace is all about. The God of love, who goes before us and seeks us out, is offering to us a new relationship—a relationship exemplified by love, forgiveness, acceptance, personal and social transformation. We may be running away from God but God is still seeking, still calling our names, still desiring to woo us through the grace of Jesus Christ.

Prevenient grace doesn't save us; rather, it comes before *anything* that we do, searching us out, calling us, wooing us, drawing us toward God, making us *want* to come to God, and enabling us to repent of our sin and exercise faith in Jesus Christ. Prevenient grace is universal in that every human being receives it. In the first epistle of John we learn that:

> [Jesus] is the atoning sacrifice for our sins, and not for
> ours only but also for the sins of the whole world.[16]

---

[16] 1 John 2:2

All grace flows from the cross, and when it is prevenient it is universal in scope and application. Human beings receive sufficient grace not only to recognize their need for God, but also to turn and accept the relationship that God is offering; this grace comes to us before we can do anything, awakening and empowering within us the desire and ability to turn. Prior to anything that we might do, prior to any act of faith or any good work, God is already working within us, molding us and moving us toward contrition, repentance, and faith.

Unfortunately, not all will repent. All, at least initially, receive the grace which brings a longing and a hunger for the divine presence in their lives, but not all will respond to this gift. All receive the gift, and all are enabled to respond, but not all will respond. Even though it is the only aspect of our Lord's work on the cross which *every* human being receives, responding to this gift is still our responsibility.

There are many denominations which share this understanding of prevenient grace. Those churches that are Anglican and Catholic in origin, theology, and practice are among those that have statements about the nature of prevenient grace in their doctrinal confessions. Other denominations have adopted similar affirmations of the initial work of the grace of God in the Christian life. While the terminology sometimes varies from that used here, the ideas are largely the same: God is the primary, initial, essential actor in our salvation; we are called, and enabled, to respond with faith.

An excellent example of a doctrinal statement affirming prevenient grace can be found in the Articles of Religion of the Church of England, which are also incorporated within the Doctrinal Standards of *The Book of Discipline* of The United Methodist Church:

> The condition of man after the fall of Adam is such
> that he cannot turn and prepare himself, by his own
> natural strength and works, to faith, and calling upon
> God; wherefore we have no power to do good works,
> pleasant and acceptable to God, without the grace
> of God by Christ preventing us, that we may have a

good will, and working with us, when we have that good will.[17]

When we assert that God begins our journey by coming to us before we do anything, what we are doing is affirming that we cannot save ourselves; we are powerless to do anything without God's initial intervention in our lives. We might think that we are the ones who have decided to seek out God, but in reality that desire comes to us from God before *we* do anything at all. We do not have, as a natural part of ourselves, a desire to know God. That desire is God's wonderful gift to all humans, apart from which no one would ever realize their need for grace, or even desire to come into God's presence.

This idea stands in stark contradiction to the ideas proposed by a group of Christians called the Pelagians, who believed that all people have the natural ability, the natural free will, to say yes to God and then to actually obey God's law and do God's will. According to the Pelagians, there is nothing fundamentally wrong with humans that needs be corrected prior to our being able to respond to God. From the Pelagian perspective, humans don't need anything special—no reconstruction, no repair work, no transformation, no regeneration, no grace—in order to obey God. The desire and ability to come to God and do God's will is thought of as being a part of who we still are. The fall doesn't bequeath to us anything more than a bad example; sin isn't part of our nature as a fundamental fault in our being, it is simply those bad things that we do. According to the Pelagians, all we need is the good example of Jesus Christ to counteract the bad example of Adam and Eve. This good example teaches us what we should do and how we should live, and it is entirely within our capacity as moral agents to follow the example of Christ. In other words, while

---

17   *The Book of Discipline of The United Methodist Church* (Nashville: The United Methodist Publishing House, 2012), 63, Article VIII

grace is a nice blessing for those who follow the right example, it is not needed to inspire, empower, or enable Christian living.[18]

Most Protestant and Roman Catholic Christians reject this approach. For the larger portion of the Christian community, grace is the bedrock upon which eternal life is built. No matter what terms are used and no matter how the ideas are presented, grace is understood to be the foundation of Christian faith and action. This is true for the beginning of the Christian walk and for every point and every stage throughout the journey.

As stated previously, prevenient grace flows from the universal atonement of Christ. The gift is universal in that, when Jesus died for the sins of the whole world *everyone* was enabled to turn to God. This gift does not involve entire regeneration, however, because it does not save. It is the first step in the regenerative process, but it is not justification. Indeed, the universal atonement neither means nor implies universal salvation precisely because the effects of the cross pertaining to salvation—the application of the blood of Jesus in payment for sin—do not occur automatically but, rather, come in response to faith.[19] In other words, universal atonement functions within the continuum of our response to the cross. In this respect, it is important to differentiate between grace in prevenience and grace in justification: prevenient grace is the stage of grace which enables our response, but which does not forgive sin and does not save. It leads to conviction of sin and enables faith, but it does not compel our faith-response. Saving grace, which will be the subject of the next section, is the stage of grace which actually forgives sin and does save: it is justification in its most basic sense. Prevenient grace suspends the affect of the fall upon the human will, enabling us to conform sufficiently to God's will that we can turn to God. Saving grace, on the other hand, eradicates the guilt and the immediate affects of the fall by placing within the believer God's regenerating,

---

[18]   Harold O. J. Brown, *Heresies: The Image of Christ in the Mirror of Heresy and Orthodoxy from the Apostles to the Present* (Garden City: Doubleday & Co, Inc., 1984), 200–202.

[19]   Romans 3:25

life-transforming presence. The difference between the two stages of grace is wholly within the recipient. They look different and have different effects because they impact the believer at different points in the believer's journey: one prior to faith, the other following faith.

Prevenient grace manifests itself in many ways. God protects us, providentially guides us, convicts us of sin, and imparts to us not only the desire but also the ability to both repent and exercise faith in Jesus Christ. One of the most obvious ways that we can sense the operation of prevenient grace is through the empowering of our conscience. An important function of our conscience is our self-awareness with respect to our relationship (or lack thereof) with God. Often theology refers to this self-awareness as the "awakening" of the soul. When we speak of such an "awakening," we are actually specifying the work of the Holy Spirit that arouses our awareness of sin, our accountability before God, and our need for forgiveness, salvation, and sanctification. Wesleyan-Arminianism asserts that without God's enablement we would not be conscious of our sin or of our need for divine grace. Nor do we have any ability to turn to God by our own initiative. In one of his sermons, John Wesley gave particular attention to the work of prevenient grace in our consciences:

> No man living is entirely destitute of what is vulgarly called natural conscience. But this is not natural; it is more properly termed preventing grace. Every man has a greater or less measure of this, which waiteth not for the call of man.[20]

Wesleyan-Arminian theology holds that human conscience is no longer a natural attribute; such an awareness of our inadequacy is actually created within us by the prevenient working of God's grace. This realization affirms the total destructive nature of the fall. As

---

[20] John Wesley, Sermon 85, "On Working Out Our Own Salvation," in *Sermons III*, ed. Albert C. Outler, vol. 3 of *The Bicentennial Edition of the Works of John Wesley* (Nashville: Abingdon Press, 1976–), 207.

fallen creatures, totally destitute of spiritual awareness, we lack even the ability to be aware of what we lack. Only through grace, preveniently functioning to enlighten our awareness, can we come to a realization that we need God. Furthermore, unempowered, unaided human insight cannot comprehend the truth of God. Our finitude is an insurmountable barrier to our acquiring any direct, absolute knowledge of an infinite God and our fallen, sinful nature renders us unworthy to come into God's presence. Unassisted by grace, we can only plunge into greater and greater confusion regarding spiritual reality. Unempowered by grace, we only have the choice of which sins to commit, never the option of "a more excellent way"—a life of faith. Only through the prior work of God can we ever come to know Christ.[21] As Paul wrote to the Church in Corinth:

> Those who are unspiritual do not receive the gifts
> of God's Spirit, for they are foolishness to them, and
> they are unable to understand them because they are
> spiritually discerned.[22]

Through prevenient grace God says "yes" to us. This initial gift of grace fills us with the desire and the ability to come to know God. We may not be aware of the gift, or we may try to deny that the gift is true and present; this is always a temptation. But, if we are honest with ourselves and open to the prompting of the Holy Spirit, we can trust that we *will* recognize our need for God and the startling truth of God's calling in our lives. I frequently have people ask me: "How do I know that God has said yes to me?" My response is a simple one: "If you're worried about it, then that's all the indicator that you need." In other words, apart from God's calling, none of us would even bother worrying about God. For some reason, not everyone recognizes the call, not everyone hears God's "yes," and in those moments all that

---

[21]   2 Corinthians 4:4; Ephesians 4:18
[22]   1 Corinthians 2:14

we can do is trust that God's ways are not our ways, and God's call comes to us when God knows that we are ready. However, if we listen with inward ears of faith, and desire to hear the good shepherd calling our names, we can trust that we *will* hear God say "yes" to us. When we hear God's call, we can also trust that we will be empowered to offer to God our response of faith by saying "yes" to God's love and presence. Prevenient grace doesn't *make* us say "yes," but it does open our ears to God's "yes" and enables our "yes" response. Through prevenient grace we are given the wonderful opportunity to respond, with faith, to the death and resurrection of Jesus Christ; but, without our willing response, nothing further happens.

This response, this saying "yes," is the next step in the Christian journey.

Justifying Grace

"All have sinned and fall short of the glory of God ...[we] are now justified by his grace as a gift, through the redemption that is in Christ Jesus, whom God put forward as a sacrifice of atonement by his blood, effective through faith."
—*Romans 3: 22b-25*

God's grace woos us, draws us, calls us to turn to Christ Jesus, to recognize our need of forgiveness, to confess our sins and say "yes" to God's love. This act of faith is our response to the good news that our Lord died on the cross for our sins, and it is enabled by the gift of prevenient grace. Prevenient grace doesn't force us to confess our sins; there is no compulsion to respond to the gift of God's grace— grace *is* resistible, inasmuch as once we have received the ability to say "yes," we *can* still say "no." Our response of faith is entirely up to us. We cannot say "yes" to God's unconditional love without God's grace first moving us, but God will not compel us to respond once grace has been applied. We can choose not to respond, we can continue rejecting God's love and the relationship that God offers us, we can deny the calling that God has on our lives and continue doing things our own way rather than God's way. This is our natural inclination—for "all we like sheep have gone astray; we have all turned everyone to our own way"[23]—but God doesn't give up on us. God is the "hound of heaven,"[24] who persistently pursues us even despite our predilection toward rejection. We can ignore God and continue in our rebellion against God's will, or we can look within ourselves, recognize our need for God's love, and say "yes" to the Divine calling.

Once we've said "yes" to our Lord's unconditional love, the next step into faith takes us into contrition. Contrition is "grieving about and being sorry for one's sins." Contrition is the state that grace produces within us when we become aware of our separation from God and our radical need for forgiveness. Comprehension of this state frequently comes to us through a period of self-examination and preparation, in which we consider both our willful acts of rebellion and our stubborn refusal to accept God's amazing love. When we consider our fallen condition, and our desperate need for God's grace, our desire to be brought into a relationship with Jesus is sparked and fueled by the Holy Spirit. Wesley termed this experience "Convicting Grace"—as we respond to God's call, and come to desire a new life in the real presence of Jesus, we are convicted by our sins and are urged to seek God's love and forgiveness.

One of the few modern spiritual writers to deal with this subject at any great length was Richard Meux Benson, the Anglican priest who, in the nineteenth century, re-established English Monasticism. Father Benson was a man of rare spiritual insight and amazing pastoral presence. His writings are not well known in the United States, but his leadership and vision in founding the Society of Saint John the Evangelist has left his mark on many thousands of people

---

[23]   Isaiah 53:6a
[24]   Francis Thompson, "The Hound of Heaven" in *The Oxford Book of English Mystical Verse.* (Oxford: Oxford University Press, 1917).

all around the world, laity and clergy alike.[25] Regarding contrition, Benson wrote:

> Our sins separate us from God because they stop up our capacity for receiving. And however much God may give, until our sins have been taken away, the receptive power of our nature remains clogged. We cannot drink in the gift of God.[26]

God does not withhold the gift of forgiveness; it's just that *we* cannot receive the gift until *we* are ready. And we can only be truly ready when we experience contrition for our sins. When we do, we demonstrate that we understand and accept how far we have separated ourselves from God, and that it is God *alone* who can bridge the gap.

Contrition is not a simple bemoaning of how horribly we have failed God. If it were that simple, salvation would come long before our faith; we would all be saved the moment we felt bad about our sins. No, in our feeble attempts to achieve contrition we may, and quite often do, find human elements of sorrow, anger and indignation; all of these feelings must be put aside before we can come to the real *joy* of true contrition. As Fr. Benson says in yet another sermon: "Contrition should result in the filling of our whole being with the joyous consciousness of divine love."[27]

In other words, being sorry for our sins should produce in us a substantial realization of God's immediate, forgiving, and life transforming love. This divine love penetrates the darkness of our sin-sick souls, revealing the glorious gospel truth that God, in Jesus Christ, has bridged the gap that we have created between God and us. Contrition is an awareness of the powerful reality of the love of God, a love that went to the cross to die in our place.

---

[25] Martin Smith, ed., *Benson of Cowley* (Cambridge: Cowley Publications, 1983), 1–16.

[26] Richard Meux Benson, *Look To The Glory* (Cambridge: Cowley Press, Reprint 1965), 44.

[27] ibid., 46.

Contrition leads to confession of sin and profession of faith. When we confess our sins before God we do so with the recognition that we cannot overcome this life-destroying nature that is a part of our being. We confess that we are at the complete mercy of God, dependent upon grace alone for forgiveness and a new life in Christ. And, in this confession, we profess our faith in Jesus Christ, who took our place when he died upon the cross for our sins and took our sins away. In our profession of faith we are saying "yes" to the love of God, "yes" to the forgiveness, and "yes" to a new and eternal relationship with Christ Jesus as our Lord and Savior.

Saying "yes" to Jesus is an *act* of faith. Faith is not *just* our mental assent to the truth of the Gospel, nor is it even *just* saying, "I believe that Jesus Christ is Lord." Assent to right doctrine and simple, passive belief are fundamentally insufficient for salvation because, as James wrote, "Faith without works is dead."[28] Indeed, two verses later James tells us *why* faith without action is dead: "Even the demons believe—and shudder."[29]

Saving faith is an *action;* it is a *way* of life. Faith without action isn't even faith—it is a dead belief that has no value and no purpose. In Biblical Greek saving faith is the verb:

$$\pi\iota\sigma\tau\varepsilon\acute{\upsilon}\omega$$

Pronounced "pisteuo," it means "an action, based upon belief grounded in confidence."[30] John Wesley, being a scholar of languages, defined it as being "trust and confidence," all the while knowing that a trust and a confidence that is passive is a trust that is cold and a confidence that is empty.[31]

---

[28] James 2:17
[29] James 2:19
[30] Bauer, 660–662
[31] Langford, p. 31.

Faith is focused, active trust in the love and presence of Christ in our lives. Faith is the tenacious act of taking one's trust and placing it not in oneself, but in the grace and strength of God as revealed to us through scripture, interpreted for us through tradition, lived through experience, and articulated through reason. When we act with faith in Jesus Christ, trusting that he has already saved us, we are living out our realization that we cannot save ourselves. We are living in the shadow of our Lord, trusting in his grace and peace.

When we say "yes" to Jesus Christ as Lord and Savior we receive justifying grace, which wipes away the guilt of our sin and incorporates us into the Body of Christ. Through justifying grace the perfect righteousness of the Lord is ascribed to us and, even though we are still guilty of sin—even though we are still sinners— God nevertheless declares us "not guilty." This is known as *imputed* righteousness: in the mind of God we are considered to be, and in fact are, treated as if we have the righteousness of Christ.

I like to look upon justification as being similar to what happens when I click on "justify margins" in my word processing application. When I do this, the margins of my text line up on either side as governed by a ruler at the top and bottom of the page, just like the margins in this book. When the text is allowed to go unjustified the effect is sloppy, uncontrolled, and unprofessional; when the text is justified the effect is clean, pleasing, and professional. Likewise, when grace justifies us we line up with God's rule. While we sometimes still run over the margins, God's grace corrects us, and over time and through the love of Jesus Christ, we gain greater degrees of proficiency at living within the rule.

And this is what Sanctifying Grace is all about.

Sanctifying Grace

"If the Spirit of him who raised Jesus from the dead dwells in you,
he who raised Christ from the dead will give life to your mortal bodies also
through his Spirit that dwells in you."
—Romans 8:11

I learned much about the nature of sanctifying grace by watching my cat, a full-blooded Maine Coon whom I named Bishop Tiggert.[32] My feline companion was given to me in 1990 by a member of the congregation at Temperance Hall United Methodist Church in eastern North Carolina, where I served as Student Pastor during my Seminary years. Fortunately for me, Tiggert's mommy and daddy were brother and sister, which made him unfit as a "show cat" but the perfect gift for a single pastor; there was no other way that I could have afforded a full-blooded Maine Coon! While Tiggert had all of the personality and most of the physical characteristics of a Maine Coon, he was nevertheless small for his breed due to his heritage, and that was why I got him for free. None of his brothers and sisters from that litter made it out of kittenhood, but Tiggert did, as lively and as wild as ever.

He was very much a "Methodist" cat—there was a method to his madness and he appeared to go about his existence in a very methodical way. He knew how to annoy me, how to please me, and how to get out of me exactly what he wanted. As my mother liked to say, Tiggert had me wrapped around his little paw.

For example, Tiggert knew that I hate to be annoyed while sleeping. And, he knew that nothing is more annoying to me during the dead quiet of the middle of the night than to hear little sounds echoing forth from the distant reaches of the house. Indeed, even just the sound of a paw gently padding against the bathroom cabinets

---

[32]   After Bishop John J. Tigert (1856–1906), the most influential scholar of Methodist polity in the later half of the 19th century and the author of the seminal text: *A Constitutional History of American Episcopal Methodism.*

can be enough to get me up, out of bed, and attending to "His Fuzzy Britches'" needs.

One night, Tiggert took up racing through the house: from the living room down the hall to my bedroom, up onto my bed where he would tag my foot, then off the bed and back up the hall to the living room. There, he would meow loudly, make some rustling noises, and then head back through the house and down the hall for my bedroom, my bed, and my foot. After about five or six rounds of this "let's pester Daddy" routine I said to myself, "one more time, and I'm putting a stop to this."

The silence was deafening. Perhaps the little beast had given up? I sighed and rolled over, content to let supposedly quiescent cats be. But, then, far away in the silence, I could hear the rumble of Tiggert's paws, racing down the hallway toward my bedroom. The sound rounded the corner, came into the room, and then ceased as Tiggert went airborne onto my bed where he padded and nibbled my left foot for a moment before darting off the bed, out the door, and up the hall. In the quiet dark of the night his scampering sounded like a whole herd of wildebeests had invaded the parsonage.

There was only one way to put a stop to this nonsense and so, even though I hated doing it, I finally got up and closed the bedroom door. Then, collapsing back onto my bed, I closed my eyes and started to drift back to sleep.

Several minutes later the rumbling sound of Tiggert's dash down the hall reached me in my groggy haze just before a loud *THWACK!* against the bedroom door jerked me fully awake. With a bit of concern, I got up and opened the door only to find Tiggert standing there with the most bemused, not to mention dazed, expression on his cute little face. Chuckling at my cat for having knocked himself silly, I scooped him up into my arms and went back to bed. Tiggert, in his brain-jarred state, would just have to settle for snuggling with Daddy.

The application of this story to the role of sanctifying grace in the Christian life is clear. Apart from the presence of the Holy Spirit in our lives we can get bull-headed about what *we* want. We can be demanding, annoying, and altogether unreasonable. We can employ devious tactics to get *our* way, despite the needs and opinions of others, ignoring even the will of God! And, we can sometimes even fool ourselves into believing that we can have things all our own way. But in the end, our schemes usually end up knocking us silly.

When we ignore the power and presence of the sanctifying grace of the Holy Spirit, all we eventually end up doing is smacking ourselves silly against the doors which God closes before us. I mean, who are we to be bull-headed, demanding, and insistent with God? Who do we think we are, pestering the Almighty like we do? How dare we go charging down God's hallway and bounding up onto God's bed to demand our own way? If we're not careful, we too will knock ourselves silly, if not knock ourselves out eternally.

God loves us and cares for us and knows what is best for us. And, yet, we frequently knock ourselves out trying to get our own way. Living by the sanctifying grace of God is all about letting go of the illusion that we are ever in control of our spiritual lives and allowing God's will to govern and transform us. It is this very transformation that makes up the greater portion of the Christian life. In other words, the Christian life isn't about just being saved; it is about *living* in the real presence of Jesus.

Contrary to what one hears in many evangelical churches, justification by grace through faith in Jesus Christ is neither the objective of one's Christian walk, nor is it the principle purpose for preaching, teaching, or spiritual formation. Quite the contrary, salvation is but the beginning of the Christian journey with God. One hasn't "arrived" when one is justified—one has only just set forth on an eternal journey with God.

As was stated earlier, justification is the point at which God declares us to be "as *though* we were Christ." The perfection, the holiness, the righteousness of Jesus is not yet an actual *part* of who we are, even though we are viewed by God as *though* we are righteous. Sanctifying grace makes God's outward declaration of our being "righteous" actually *part* of our inward reality. In the terms of the above story about my cat, sanctifying grace leads us in recognizing that it's better to be asleep in the crook of our Lord's arm than to be pestering God and giving ourselves metaphorical headaches in the process.

Romans 8:11 affirms this truth as it asserts that the Holy Spirit, who raised Jesus from the dead, also raises us from the death of our sins to new life in Christ Jesus. We are not left to our own devices, our own wills, our own plans; we are granted the same power that raised Jesus, a power that can truly transform us from the death of our sins to Jesus' eternal life.

In theological circles this is known as *imparted* righteousness. The grace of Jesus Christ, living and moving in us through the power and presence of the Holy Spirit, doesn't leave us in a sinning state; rather, it takes an active role in transforming us so that we become more like Jesus. Sanctifying grace takes the *imputed* righteousness of justifying grace and applies it to us in such a way that we are not only judged by God *as though* we are righteous, but over time we actually take on more and more of the righteousness of Christ. *Imparted* righteousness is "imparted" *precisely* in that it becomes a part of who we are.

This can be seen in the way in which the Lord dealt with Peter:

> When they had finished breakfast, Jesus said to Simon Peter, "Simon son of John, do you love me more than these?" He said to him, "Yes, Lord; you know that I love you." Jesus said to him, "Feed my lambs." A second time he said to him, "Simon son of John, do you love me?" He said to him, "Yes, Lord; you know that I love you." Jesus said to him, "Tend my sheep." He said to him the third time, "Simon son of John, do you love me?" Peter felt hurt because he said to him the third time, "Do you love me?" And he said to him, "Lord, you know everything; you know that I love you." Jesus said to him, "Feed my sheep.[33]

---

[33]   John 21:15-17

While not readily apparent in the English translation, in the Greek the movement from the divine to the human perspective is striking. Three times Jesus asked Peter if he loved him. The first two times he asked the question, Jesus used the ultimate, divine form of the Greek word for love: *agape*. Each time, Peter's response was not with this divine form of love, but with the brotherly form of love: *phileo*. It's as if each time Jesus asked: "Do you love me?" Peter's response was: "Yes, Lord, you know that I like you." Twice Peter showed that he didn't have the ability to respond to Jesus with the unlimited, divine, self-giving love that Jesus was searching for in Peter's heart. The good news for Peter, and for us, comes in the fact that Jesus didn't just drop the fisherman and turn to another disciple, nor did Jesus just leave him with *phileo* love. No, our Lord stooped down to where Peter was and asked him "Do you love [*phileo*] me?" Jesus was willing to reach down to where Peter was, at that specific point in his life, and relate with him in a way that this rugged fisherman could accept. And, yet again, Peter's response was, "Lord, you know everything; you know that I love [*phileo*] you." The element of sanctifying grace in all of this is that Jesus didn't leave Peter in the state of being able to share only *phileo* love. No, much later on in his life we discover that Peter had grown in grace to the point where he was able to write:

> Although you have not seen him [Jesus], you love him; and even though you do not see him now, you believe in him and rejoice with an indescribable and glorious joy, for you are receiving the outcome of your faith, the salvation of your souls.[34]

Here, the apostle uses the word *agape*, asserting that even those who had never seen Jesus love him—a love that Peter, who *had* seen Jesus, had been slow to discover in himself.

Sanctifying grace imparts to us the righteousness of Christ. God's perfect love is, through our openness to the Holy Spirit, made

---

[34]   1 Peter 1:8

an inexorably increasing part of who and what we are. We become *more* and *more* like Jesus. In other words, the Love and Will of God in Jesus Christ, communicated to us through the person and work of the Holy Spirit, becomes engrafted within us and we are transformed. We don't produce this transformation on our own; it is entirely the work of the Holy Spirit, refashioning us in the perfect love of Christ.

Perfection

"I am confident of this; that the one who began a good work among you will bring it to completion by the day of Jesus Christ."
—*Philippians 1:6*

The story may be apocryphal, or perhaps it is true, but whatever the case may be, the story goes that one night a Presbyterian minister was preaching a revival sermon at a Methodist Church. Thinking he had a captive audience, he decided to score a few theological points. So, in the middle of his sermon, he paused to ask, "You Methodists believe that you're all moving on toward perfection; so, tell me, are there any in the house tonight who believe that they're perfect?"

In the back of the congregation a middle-aged woman stood up, drawing the attention of all in the sanctuary.

The Presbyterian minister, hardly able to believe his eyes, cleared his throat and asked in an incredulous tone: "Yes, sister? Are *you* perfect?"

The lady looked around self-consciously at those seated near her, and then she braced her shoulders, held her head up high and said, "No, sir ... but my husband's first wife was."[35]

Laughter is supposed to follow.

---

[35] This originated with Henry Ward Beecher (1813–1887), the 19th century "Prince of the Pulpit" who was well known for his wit, sagacity, and social activism. See: Debby Applegate, *The Most famous Man in America: The Biography of Henry Ward Beecher* (New York: Doubleday Religious Publishing Group, 2006).

This story is funny because it highlights the innate discomfort that most of us have with the idea of perfection. We are acutely aware that we are very far from being perfect; even though we may put an extraordinary amount of effort into trying to live as God would have us to live, we know that we fail, and do it miserably, every time we try. And, yet, we also know that our Lord was abundantly clear on this subject:

"Be perfect, therefore, as your heavenly Father is perfect."[36]

Perfect? Jesus expects us to be perfect? Exactly! We're expected to be perfect not just as Jesus is perfect, but as the "heavenly Father is perfect." While we may know people who are extraordinarily good, who are kind and gentle-hearted, who are always ready to help in time of need, who are present to speak a word of comfort and express God's love to all, who even make it their life's devotion to care for the needy, the hungry, the poor, the homeless, the sick, and others who are disadvantaged, it is an absolute certainty that none of us knows anybody who is perfect. Or do we?

What does it mean to be perfect? Is perfection being without fault or blemish, entirely lacking in sin or self-will? Yes, all of these ideas describe what perfection looks like; but true, spiritual perfection is far more than any of these things. The Greek word that is usually translated into English as "perfect" is:

$$\tau \acute{\epsilon} \lambda o \varsigma$$

Pronounced *telos*, fundamentally it means the "end" or the "goal" toward which one strives.[37] It means to "complete," "fulfill," "succeed," or "attain maturity." In other words, things are *telos*—things are

---

[36]   Matthew 5:48
[37]   Bauer, 811–812.

perfect—when they have reached their fullness, their maturity, their complete purpose, goal, and objective. While being without sin is a critical element within what it means to be perfect, for us to limit the meaning of perfection to just that objective is to limit its meaning far beyond either its theological or its biblical scope. Being perfect is about forensic, spiritual, emotional, and experiential maturity. It is about attaining the objective that God has for us: the "putting on of Christ."[38]

While none of us can be perfect by our *own* ability, Wesleyan-Arminianism affirms that through God's sanctifying grace we *can be* transformed into progressively greater likenesses of Christ. As we grow in faith, and as grace works its sanctifying miracle within us, we find ourselves approaching full communion with the Will of God and, in Glory if nowhere else, we can trust that we *will* be made perfect even as Jesus is perfect. To help us along the way toward the perfect love of Christ, we are granted the joy of being blessed by occasional moments—fleeting instances—of true holiness: moments in which we know that we are living in God's perfect love and Will. This has been the experience of many Christians who, by no virtue of their own, have discovered themselves immersed in the real presence of Jesus. When we exercise the many means of grace[39] we come to know that we are in the all encompassing, life transforming, soul confirming, perfect love of God. While still being far from perfect ourselves, we nevertheless can attain a fleeting experience of what God's perfect love is like; this experience ignites within us a hunger and thirst for more grace, more faith, and more holiness. It is like an appetizer of God's love, given to us when we engage in a faithful response to God's grace. It is a pure manifestation of the hope of glory which we are promised in Christ Jesus our Lord. And, it is an experience which all Christians can have.

This is what John Wesley intended when he said that we are all to be "moving on toward perfection." He had no illusions of such being

---

[38]   Romans 13:14
[39]   For example: reading scripture, praying, singing hymns and songs of faith, partaking of Holy Communion.

our own doing; Wesley consistently understood sanctification and perfection as the work of the grace of God, transforming us through the power of the Holy Spirit. As Thomas Langford summarized it:

> The fruition of sanctification is conformity to the mind of Christ; always, for Wesley, the Holy Spirit reinforces our life in Christ. Christian perfection is progressive, a continual renewal of love and growth in love. Both realized and being realized, it is a love that matures into greater love.[40]

"… it is love that matures into greater love." This concept cannot be minimized. When Wesleyans speak about Christian perfection they're not just talking about freedom from specific sins. While transformation of this form is also part of the sanctifying experience, what makes the movement toward holiness possible is the all-infusing and life-transforming love of God.

Total perfection in love is possible—if only for those few instants where we are graced to know the perfect love of God in our lives. At the same time, we should realize that we are always going to be struggling against sin. However, we can be assured that, if we persevere in the faith, we will be entirely transformed in glory, incapable of sin and released for eternal, perfect love in Jesus Christ. The joyous news is that we are occasionally encouraged in our spiritual walk by finding ourselves, from time to time, entering into a periodic and temporary state of perfect conformity to the Will of God. These moments of God's perfection overcome our human sin and give us a foretaste of what life free from the constraints of this mortal existence holds in store for us.

And, it is all of grace.

---

[40]   Langford, 40-42.

Questions for Reflection and Discussion

Chapter Two

♦ What do the letters T.U.L.I.P. stand for?

♦ What do you think about each of these points? Do any of them make you feel uncomfortable? If so, why? If not, why not?

♦ How would you respond to the following statement?

> *I'm saved, and I can't lose it, so why should I live a Christian life? Let's go to Las Vegas and just have fun! Being a Christian doesn't matter anyway ... God has already saved those whom God wants!"*

♦ What are the differences between Calvinists and Arminians?

♦ What is prevenient grace? How do you see it moving in your life? Describe those people, events, ideas, and things that have directed you to the love of God in the past.

♦ What is justifying grace? When were you justified? Describe what it felt like when you first realized that you were "saved."

♦ If the moment of your justification cannot be identified—if you can't put your finger on the precise instance of your salvation— give some thought to the development of your relationship with Christ from childhood to adulthood. Consider those moments when you knew that God had forgiven specific sins in your life, and describe what it felt like to be forgiven.

◆ What is the meaning of the word "faith?" Why is it not just belief?

◆ Describe an act of faith, and identify one or more instances in your own life when you were acting in faith.

◆ What is the theological difference between *imputed* and *imparted* righteousness?

◆ What is sanctifying grace? How do you see it moving in your life?

◆ Can you identify those people or things in your life through which God may be working to transform you?

◆ What do you believe it means to be "perfect?"

◆ Describe a time in your life when you believe yourself to have been in communion with the will of God. What did it feel like to know that you were in the presence of God?

◆ Have you ever heard the voice of God, speaking to you? In that moment, was God's will for your life clear? Did you have any doubt that God loved you?

◆ What happens when you "move outside God's margins" for your life? Describe a time in your life when this happened, and consider the effects of this time on your current spiritual walk and the walk of those around you.

O Blessed Holy Spirit

O Blessed Holy Spirit
      Come to me this day
Shower on this wretched soul
      Your Grace and Peace to Stay.

From day to day I wander
      Through life's rocky ways
Without Your Holy Presence
      I know my will would stray.

Your Grace supports me everywhere
      Your Breath so fills my lungs!
My voice proclaims Your Loving Grace
      And through my voice you've sung.

O Blessed Holy Spirit
      Come to me to stay;
Fill my every waking thought
      And guide me along The Way.

Gregory S. Neal †
June 1995

Chapter Three

The Sacraments As Means of Grace

T hroughout much of Protestant Christianity there tends to be a great deal of confusion over the nature and function of Divine grace in the life of the believer. Does grace save? Does faith save? Does grace, operating through faith, save? Does grace come to us before we have faith, or after, or both? Can we reject or ignore grace, or are we free to say "no" to God? Questions like these are not new; they have raged among Christians—and not just Protestant Christians—for much of the last two millennia. As the third millennium has dawned for the Church, it doesn't appear as though we are any closer to a definitive conclusion on these matters. Those who tend more toward the catholic side of the theological continuum still see these matters from one perspective while non-sacramental Baptists, Church of Christ, and others from the Reformed community still tend to see things from an opposite point of view.

Chapter Two laid the groundwork for an approach to the nature and function of grace that is acceptable to Christians who tend to gravitate more toward the catholic side of the spectrum. This does not mean that those who are Baptist, Reformed, or Campbellite (i.e., Church of Christ), won't find many ideas and concepts that they share with the discussion on the stages of grace. Quite the contrary, one of the beautiful things about systematic theology is that elements from one system are often found, perhaps with a different terminology, spread across multiple contradictory systems. This, I believe, is a manifestation of the fact that even though we certainly disagree on many matters, we *do* still worship the very same Lord and Savior. If we can keep our disagreements in this perspective, perhaps there is hope for the future unity of the Body of Christ. It certainly has not been my intention to say that alternative approaches to the stages of grace in the Christian life are wrong. Instead, the groundwork was laid in Chapter Two for the purpose of asking the following question:

> "How does one receive God's prevenient, justifying, sanctifying, and perfecting grace?"

Those who approach this question from the catholic side of the theological spectrum will tend to answer these questions one way, while those who come from the reformed tradition will gravitate toward a different set of responses. It is this very difference that, more than anything else, characterizes each group.

I am frequently asked, "What is the difference between Methodists and Baptists?" While this question depends upon two stereotypes (one for Baptists and one for Methodists), it is a valid question, particularly within the context of this book. In general, Methodists affirm that grace comes to us through instrumental means; Baptists, on the other hand, tend to affirm that grace is either neutral toward instrumental means or entirely independent from them. Some are surprised to learn that this difference in approach is the most important one between Methodists and Baptists. Sure, there are many other differences, but most of the more obvious ones—like forms of church government—flow from this difference in perspective. How one interprets the receipt of grace affects everything that one does in the Christian life.

For example, if you believe that instrumental means are the normal channels through which grace comes to you, you're going to be rather more diligent in availing yourself of those means than you would be if you didn't believe that grace comes through instrumentalities. Those who prefer the perspective of ordinance theology do still consider the means of grace to be important—they are the principle foci around which the community of the faith gathers for worship—but they are not *instrumental* in the receipt of grace. Since they are not instrumental, they can easily be left out of the picture if time doesn't allow or conditions make them inconvenient. In other words, they become optional relative to the issue of one's receipt of grace.

This doesn't mean that they are optional relative to one's duty to observe them. Quite the contrary, those who prefer the ordinance approach do still consider them to be, if not instrumental means of grace, at least means by which we express our love and obedience to the Will of God. After all, Christ did ordain that we observe them and so, even if they don't function instrumentally in the receipt of grace, those who follow ordinance theology are not at any liberty to simply reject or ignore them.

Again, I want to assert that this should not be taken in any way as an attack upon non-sacramental approaches to the means of grace. It is simply a fact that the opinion of those on the reformed side of the spectrum differs from the opinion of those on the catholic side of the spectrum. This is not necessarily a bad thing; God uses many different genres, nuances, and images to communicate the truth of the Divine presence in the life of the Church. Some people are drawn by, and derive meaning from, the concept of receiving grace through instrumental means, while others tend to view grace as being present apart from instrumentality. I believe that this diversity of opinion is a *good* thing.

In Chapter One we examined the nature and means of grace. To summarize, there are many different means of grace: while some of them are certainly more familiar than others, one of the fundamental claims of sacramental theology is that *anything* which serves to convey the love and real presence of our Lord Jesus Christ to the believer can be understood as a means of grace. This is true for the traditional instruments—the sacraments and the other sacramental acts which have been instituted by the Church over the past two thousand years—as well as for what would appear to be the simple, mundane elements of our everyday living. A cup of water or a hot meal can be a means of grace to a person who has neither. A jacket, a hug, and a kind word, or even just a pleasant smile, can all serve as instruments through which someone in need, loneliness, or despair might receive the grace of God. Anything can be a means of grace.

Indeed, I am convinced that *everything* is a means of grace. This goes for both good things and bad things, good experiences and bad experiences, good feelings and bad feelings, joys and pains, hopes and disappointments—in and through *all* things, God's grace can be found if only we have the eyes of faith to look and recognize it. The Apostle Paul was convinced of this truth:

> We know that all things work together for good for those who love God, who are called according to his purpose.[41]

This doesn't mean that everyone, in every circumstance, will see, know, and receive God's grace; indeed, in the midst of painful experiences it can be particularly difficult to comprehend the presence of God in all things. It usually takes patient discernment to identify the hand of God moving in tragic circumstances, and it is certainly true that the pain can become so great, and the disappointment so stark, that even the well-honed discernment of mature Christians cannot always apprehend God's presence in difficult times.

Nevertheless, it has been the experience of many that given time for healing, reflection, and prayer, it is possible to see God's presence even in the midst of horrific events. This does *not* mean that God causes such tragedies; God doesn't shoot children in public schools, or drag innocent men to death behind pickup trucks, or murder homosexual youth—God doesn't do any of these things, nor does God approve of them. And, yet, even amidst the evils of this life, even through the tears and the pain that can come with living, God

---

[41]   Romans 8:28

can still be discerned and grace can still be received even when it is not known or felt to be present *at the time.*

Looking back upon the difficult periods in my own life and ministry, I can see that the love of God was always present with me in many different ways and through many different people. Even when I was in the darkest valley—in the midst of my pastorate at the "First Church of Hell"—the means of grace were frequently near me and signs of God's love could be discerned somewhere in my life. This is true not just of those means of grace which one would expect, like the prayers of one's family and friends, but even of the least likely of individuals.

Indeed, from my current perspective I can see that even some of those people who desired to "get rid" of me were actually, at times and despite their intentions, instruments of God's love for me. I didn't know or realize it at the time, but I wasn't alone. Even in the darkest hour, when a "clergy-killer" who was out to destroy everything that God had accomplished in my ministry directly threatened my life, I now realize that God's grace was present and working miracles. It was grace that enabled me to continue preaching, Sunday after Sunday. It was grace that lifted my hands and opened my lips as I presided at the Eucharist and offered the bread of heaven. It was grace that was present in every act of ministry, yes even to that particular individual sitting in the pew, glaring darts of venom and hatred at me, an individual for whom Jesus died just as assuredly as he died for me. True, at the time it was painful to continue in that pastorate, but today I can look back and see that Jesus was present and active in many unexpected ways. Today I can look back and realize that, despite how I might have felt while in the deepest, darkest valley of my ministry, I wasn't bereft of the love and power of God.

Given time, prayer, and much reflection, I believe that *everything* can be discerned to contain at least a spark of the grace of our Lord Jesus Christ. And, as such, the means of grace can be seen in everything. The grace of God can be seen coming to us through prayer, healing, forgiveness, scripture, pastors, teachers, friends, spouses, music, and especially through water, bread, and wine.

Throughout the history of the church, Christians have identified and institutionalized many of these means of grace in the form of sacraments and other sacramental acts, each playing an important role in the lives of believers. In this chapter we will examine the nature of the sacraments and the sacramentals over and against the understanding of ordinance theology.

Defining the Sacraments

"Let us therefore approach the throne of grace with boldness,
so that we may receive mercy and find grace to help in time of need."
—Hebrews 4:16

If the means of grace are those instrumental ways that God's unmerited favor is communicated to believers, and if the sacraments are understood as being means of grace, then how are we to differentiate between the sacraments and those means which aren't sacraments? In other words, why aren't all the means of grace considered sacraments? Why don't Protestants accept, as sacraments, the clear means of grace that are available to the church in the forms of prayer, healing, confession, forgiveness, ordination, marriage, giving, or even foot- washing? Throughout the history of the Church, many of these means of grace have been recognized and institutionalized as sacraments. Most Protestants, however, tend to reject all but Baptism and Holy Communion as being truly sacraments. Why do Protestants limit the title of *sacrament* to *only* these two? Why aren't all the means of grace considered sacraments? In short, *what* is a sacrament?

The term *sacrament* is derived from the Old Latin word *sacrare,* which denotes anything that produces holiness.[42] In Roman paganism it referenced the vow or ritual action which initiated a transfer of anyone or anything from a secular standing to a position of divine right and responsibility. In other words, it was the liturgical element which produced ritual holiness in a person, place, or thing. The Latin word *sacramentum* is first found used for the Greek word μυστήριον, or "mystery," in some of the Old Latin translations of the New Testament, and as such the term came to indicate to Christians a thing which was both sacred and mysterious.[43]

The term *sacramentum* was imprecisely adopted and applied by the early Christian writers as they attempted to describe the many symbolic actions, signs, and ceremonies that functioned for them as means of grace. For example, several early Christian authors refer to "The Sacrament of the Lord's Prayer," while still others write about the "Sacrament of Labor," the "Sacrament of Service," and the "Sacrament of Worship." [44] Each of these is described and experienced as a means of grace—they all function within the life of the believer as channels through which God's love and presence is conveyed. Even though they can all be affirmed as being sacramental *in nature,* none of them are actually identifiable as sacraments. Yes, they are means of grace; no, they are *not* sacraments.

This kind of loose application of the term "sacrament" in the history of the Church led to the conclusion that, unless there were going to be thousands of sacraments, a far more precise definition than just "mysterious and sacred things" or "means of grace" was needed. Such a definition began to take form in the theological

---

[42]   Joseph Pohle, *The Sacraments: A Dogmatic Treatise. Vol. 1, The Sacraments in General. Baptism, Confirmation* (London: B. Herder Book Co., 1946), 5.

[43]   Herbert Vorgrimler, *Sacramental Theology* (Collegeville: The Liturgical Press, 1992), 44–47.

[44]   Pohle, 7.

contemplation and articulation of such great thinkers as St. Augustine of Hippo[45], Hugh of St. Victor, and Peter Lombard.

Augustine's initial definition of "sacrament" was still vague, but it provided some controls over the multiplication of the *sacramenta*. For Augustine, the sacraments were:

> ...visible signs that represent an invisible reality. A *sacramentum* is a *sacrum signum,* that is, a sign designated by God to point to a divine reality (*res divina*) and containing that reality within itself.[46]

This initial definition highlighted the importance of recognizing the real, effectual nature of divine grace in the sacrament, combined with a visible, exterior, physical component. In many respects, however, this is also a valid definition of the means of grace in general, not of the sacraments in particular. The use of this vague definition led Augustine to identify a multitude of sacraments—far more than was functionally manageable. The short form of Augustine's definition, one which became popular in the European theology of the early middle ages, was: *invisibulis gratiae visibilis forma,* or "the visible form of invisible grace."[47] Again, this is an excellent partial-definition of the means of grace in general, but hardly a useful definition for the sacraments.

Both Hugh of St. Victor[48] and Peter Lombard[49] sought to modify Augustine's concept of the sacraments. The product of their thinking, filtered through the voluminous work of St. Thomas Aquinas, led to

---

[45]   St. Augustine of Hippo (354–430 A.D.) was probably one of the most influential Theologians in the history of the Church. His writings had a far-reaching impact on Roman Catholic thought and on the leaders of the Protestant Reformation. He was Bishop of the Church in *Hippo Regius* (modern-day Annaba in northeastern Algeria, North Africa).

[46]   Vorgrimler, 45.

[47]   ibid.

[48]   Hugh of St. Victor (1096–1141 A.D.) was a monastic priest and leading theologian of mystical theology. His writings shaped Christian thought for centuries after his life.

[49]   Peter Lombard (abt. 1100–1164 A.D.) was an influential Theologian and the Bishop of Paris.

the following, excellent definition of a sacrament, which can be found in the Roman Catholic *Dictionary of the Liturgy:*

> Outward signs or sacred actions, instituted by Christ, through which grace is channeled or communicated for inward sanctification of the soul.[50]

The elements of this definition are worthy of special note. Firstly, a sacrament is an "outward" sign or action. It is not a quiet, invisible, personal, and private action; rather, it is a visible, objectively established representation of that which *is* invisible and internal. Secondly, a sacrament must have been a sign or an action established by Jesus. Not just any sign or action will do, not just any means of grace can be considered a sacrament. To be sacraments, Christ must have established them. Thirdly, a sacrament serves as a true method by which grace is received. In other words, sacraments are not just wishful thinking, nor are they promises, nor are they even indicators. Sacraments are *real* conduits through which the love of God is communicated to us. And, fourthly, the grace received is *transforming* in character. Fundamentally, the sacraments *sanctify* us. Or, as John Wesley might have put it: through the sacraments we encounter the grace of God, and this grace "moves us on toward perfection."

These points are reflected in the Anglican and Methodist Articles of Religion, which state in their shared Article on the topic of the Sacraments in general:

> Sacraments ordained of Christ are not only badges or tokens of Christian men's profession, but rather they are certain signs of grace, and God's good will toward us, by which he doth work invisibly in us, and doth

---

[50]   Jovian Lang, ed. *Dictionary of the Liturgy* (New York: Catholic Book Publishing Co., 1989), 561.

not only quicken, but also strengthen and confirm, our faith in him.[51]

Here, we find the sacraments defined as being not just announcements of faith, but as visual signs of the actual means of prevenient, justifying, and sanctifying grace which were established by Christ Jesus.

Based upon these definitions, the nature of the sacraments as being distinct from the other means of grace becomes evident. Those means of grace which lack one or more of the before-listed characteristics, while certainly still means of grace, are *not* sacraments. For example, worship and fellowship have strong sacramental characteristics, and they certainly are means of grace, but they are not *technically* sacraments.

The same cannot be said for several of the other means of grace which have been considered sacraments by the Roman Catholic Church. For example, while most Protestants have rejected the sacramentality of the rite of penance (a.k.a. "The Sacrament of Reconciliation"), our brothers and sisters in the Roman Catholic Church and in the Eastern Orthodox Communions have considered penance an important sacrament. And, after much reflection, I can no longer honestly say that they are wrong. There is certainly a sacramental spirituality to confession and forgiveness that cannot be denied. Indeed, the sacramental nature of Reconciliation is, in my opinion, so strong that such rites may very well be validly understood as either full-blown sacraments or, in the very least, as "sacramentals." This is particularly true when the Dominical character of confession and forgiveness is considered. Jesus certainly directed his disciples to forgive the sins of others:

---

[51]   Article XVI, The Methodist Articles of Religion, *The Book of Discipline of The United Methodist Church, 2012*; Article XXV, The Articles of Religion of the Church of England. *The Book of Common Prayer*. (New York: Seabury Press, 1979)

> If you forgive the sins of any, they are forgiven them;
> if you retain the sins of any, they are retained." [52]

Questions concerning the penitential rites, and the issue of their sacramental characteristics, will be covered in Chapter Six. For now, suffice it to say that, while Jesus established several means of grace, not all are of equal value or character. In this I am in complete agreement with my Protestant brothers and sisters: Communion and Baptism are the two *principle* means of grace and, as such, they are our sacraments. No matter what may be said in favor of the other means of grace, none of them can measure up to the powerful presence of Jesus that can be known and received in these two principle means. This tends to be the conclusion of the Anglican, Methodist, Lutheran, and other catholic but non-Roman communions. As the Anglican/ Methodist Articles of Religion state:

> Those five commonly called sacraments, that is to say, confirmation, penance, orders, matrimony, and extreme unction, are not to be counted for Sacraments of the Gospel; being such as have partly grown out of the corrupt following of the apostles, and partly are states of life allowed in the Scriptures, but yet have not the like nature of Baptism and the Lord's Supper, because they have not any visible sign or ceremony ordained of God.[53]

In short, while these five means of grace have definite scriptural justification for a role in the life of a believer, they are not understood to have the same sacramental character as Baptism and Holy Communion.

---

[52]   John 20:23. See also Matthew 18:21–35

[53]   Article XVI, The Methodist Articles of Religion, *The Book of Discipline of The United Methodist Church, 2012*; The Anglican Article reads similarly, with only a slightly different grammar.

A New Definition

> "…They are now justified by his grace as a gift, through the
> redemption that is in Christ Jesus, whom God put forward as a
> sacrifice of atonement by his blood, effective through faith."
> — *Romans 3:22b-25a*

In all of these definitions of the sacraments there seems to be
lacking an unambiguous affirmation that God is the *principle* actor.
While certainly implied in all prior statements, the differentiation
between the principle actor and the one who is acted upon is important
for clarifying the difference between a general means of grace and
a sacrament. Likewise, also lacking in the traditional definitions of
the sacraments is the importance of the human response to the grace
received. And it is *here* that I believe a strong distinction can be
drawn between the general means of grace and the sacraments. In
short, I propose the *necessity of human response* as the fundamental
characteristic that differentiates a sacrament as distinct from the
other general means of grace. Proposing this distinction has led me
to the following modification of the classic definition of a sacrament:

> A sacrament is a means of effective grace—an
> outward and visible sign of God's inward and spiritual
> favor—which is totally unoccasioned by anything
> that we do and which, furthermore, elicits a response
> of faith from the receiver in order to be completed.

It must first be noted that the principle actor in *every* means of grace
is God. Long before we do anything, God gives us grace; regardless
of our response, the means of grace impart to us God's love and favor.
This means that every means of grace, including sacramental grace,
is initially prevenient in character. We do nothing to *begin* its action
in our lives because the love of God has *already* been poured out to us

from the cross of Jesus Christ. The sacraments differ from the other means of grace, however, when it comes to our response of faith.

The general means of grace may or may not elicit a response of faith—like the seed in our Lord's parable, they may fall on our stony hearts, or on the weed-choked fields of our lives; they may not put down deep roots, the circumstances which surround us may not welcome their presence, and the heat of our sins may cause them to shrivel up and stagnate.[54] Regardless of the response of the believer, grace is still present and still plays a role in our lives. In other words, prayer works, even despite our weakness or lack of faith. This is true for all the means of grace—they work; they *always* work; they may be limited in their function by our refusal to respond, but they work nevertheless; they work even apart from our awareness that they're working. True, usually we can see, know, and accept that the means of grace are functioning, but they don't require our awareness to function any more than we need to think every time we take a breath. The means of grace simply *are*.

The sacraments, being means of grace, also communicate favor. However, for the means of grace to be completed within the sacrament— for the sanctifying effects of divine grace to be made known in our lives a response of faith *must* be forthcoming from us. God's grace is always perfect, always complete, and always present; our response, unfortunately, is not. Hence, the means of grace are sure, but their identity as completed sacraments depends upon our response of faith.

This is another place where the Protestants on the catholic side of the theological spectrum differ from their Roman Catholic sisters and brothers. Regardless of the faith of the receiver, the Roman Catholic approach views the sacraments as sure means of sanctifying grace. Protestant-Catholics[55], on the other hand, view the sacraments as

---

54   The parable of the sower, found at Matthew 13:3–9

55   I am using this term to denote Anglicans, Methodists, Lutherans, Presbyterians, and all other Protestants who are on the catholic side of the theological spectrum. They are distinct from Protestant-Separatists, who historically prefer to differentiate themselves from most of the fundamental assumptions of catholic Christianity. A rule of thumb for identifying Protestant-Catholics is the use of the historic creeds of the church in worship: if a church utilizes the creeds, they are probably Protestant-Catholics; if a church does not utilize the creeds, they are probably Protestant-Separatists.

only having power to sanctify when we employ them through faith. Without faith, while they still present the love of God to us and so embody prevenient grace, they don't produce a sanctifying change within us. The sacraments not only communicate to us effectively God's grace, but when we partake of them by faith they complete a work of God's sanctification within us. Our response of faith is required for the grace to "move us on toward perfection." Without our *response*, the sacraments are still means of grace, but they are not *completed*—they are not actualized. It is our response of faith which brings the sacraments to effective completion.

The means of grace are the tools, the instruments, the conduits through which God communicates to us divine favor. When we receive the means of grace, *even without faith,* they have an immediate prevenient impact on our lives: they, if only by virtue of the faith of others, move us closer to God. When we respond to the means of grace with faith, however, they move us even further into God's sanctifying Will for our lives. Indeed, it might even be said that it is our very response of faith that propels any of the general means of grace into the category of a "sacramental." And this is also the reason why there remains such a vague, hazy line of distinction between the sacraments and the sacramental's; faith functions in both. When the means of grace are actual sacraments, however, our response of faith brings to *completion* within us a mighty working of God's perfecting love. Be the grace justifying, sanctifying, or perfecting, when we respond with faith the sacraments truly do communicate to us the Real Presence of Almighty God.

Sacraments or Ordinances?

This way of looking at the sacraments is at odds with the ordinance-based understanding of Baptism and the Lord's Supper which is most common among the Baptist, Church of Christ, and Reformed communions.[56] Ordinance theology focuses upon the Christian's cognitive and willful act of obedience to our Lord's commandment that we baptize as expressions of our faith, and "remember him" as we eat the Lord's Supper. For them, the sacraments are memorial moments.[57]

Those who consider the sacraments to be ordinances and not means of grace frequently tend to think of their interpretation of the sacraments as being ancient and reflective of the early church's position. In point of fact, however, their approach is fairly new in the history of the Church, dating from the time of the Reformation and the teachings of such Anabaptists as Blaurock, Grebel, and Simons on the one hand, and of the Swiss Reformer Huldrych Zwingli on the other.[58] Zwingli's theology was based on a single principle, which governed much of his theological thought: if the Old or New Testament did not say something explicitly and literally, no Christian should either believe it or practice it. In 1522, for instance, Zwingli opposed the traditional practice of fasting during the liturgical season of Lent. His argument was that nowhere in the New Testament is fasting during Lent ever mentioned. Indeed, the season of Lent itself is not at all Biblical and, hence, fasting during Lent should not be practiced and the season itself should not be observed. Both were considered inherently unchristian.[59]

Concerning the sacraments, Zwingli rejected instrumentality and was entirely loath to accept or recognize any means of grace other than direct, unmediated communion with God. Sacramental causality was tantamount to blasphemy for him because such a way of accounting for the receipt of grace detracted from the immediacy of God's presence. Rather than viewing the means of grace and the sacraments as being the ways through which God's presence is

---

[56] Otherwise known as the Protestant-Separatists.
[57] Brown, 322–325.
[58] Geoffrey Bromiley, *Historical Theology: An Introduction* (Edinburgh: T&T Clark, 1978), 275–279.
[59] Brown, 324.

made known to Christians, Zwingli believed that the elements of water, bread, and wine, actually *created* barriers between God and humankind.[60] Contrary to instrumental presence, Zwingli asserted that the sacramental symbols were "tokens or emblems, like an engagement ring…."[61] They were outward symbols *only*. Rather than being a means of grace, an outward and visible sign of God's inward and spiritual grace, Zwingli argued, "…a sacrament is a confession, not a confirmation, of faith."[62] In other words, it is an "ordinance."

All of the above being said, I do want to affirm that even Zwinglian theology accepts that the grace of God is present when a Christian partakes of the ordinances. However, it must be remembered that presence is *not* understood as being mediated in any way through the ordinances themselves. The grace of God doesn't come through the instrument of prayer, or through the instrument of the scriptures, or through the instruments of water, bread, and wine. Rather, if grace is understood as being present in any proximity to the ordinances, it is present in the undefined link between the Christian and God that has, as its only manifestation, the atoning sacrifice of Jesus upon the cross. Grace flows from God directly to the believer by virtue of the work of Christ; it is not conveyed *through* instruments.

In ordinance theology, neither Baptism nor the Lord's Supper function as means of grace. The Christian doesn't receive anything of a spiritual nature (and certainly not the real presence of Jesus) through the partaking of the Lord's Supper or by receiving the waters of Baptism. In ordinance theology attention is placed upon what the believer is doing in the rite, not upon what God does. As such, ordinance theology is *entirely* dependent upon the capacity of the receiver to both understand and participate in the rite involved. Essentially, for Zwinglians the ordinances have become "good works" rather than being instrumental "means of grace." They are

---

[60]   B.A. Gerrish, *Grace and Gratitude: The Eucharistic Theology of John Calvin* (Minneapolis: Fortress Press, 1993), 164.
[61]   ibid.
[62]   ibid., 105.

not channels for receiving God's love but, rather, ways in which we express our love of, faith in, and obedience to the commandments of Christ. They are badges, or tokens, of the covenant relationship which we have with Christ, not the means by which that covenant is either established or maintained.[63]

It is this quality of ordinance theology—the focus upon the ability of the recipient and not upon the active grace of God—that has resulted in some horrific misinterpretations of Paul's directions regarding Holy Communion.[64] The outright blasphemous demand that Christians must be "worthy" in order to partake of the elements is rooted in an understanding of Communion as being something that *we* do. Granted, not all supporters of ordinance theology will fall into this trap, but it is a trap that is peculiarly "ordinance" in nature. In Chapter Five we will examine this subject in greater length.

The difference between a sacramental understanding of the means of grace and an ordinance understanding of these same rites must be recognized before the differences in interpretation of the Scriptural witness, and the subsequent traditions of the Church, can be understood. The presuppositions brought to this subject will play a large role in determining one's interpretation of the evidence. Both perspectives have Scriptural warrants for their approach, and both rely upon a specific set of hermeneutical devices and assumptions which are not organically part of the Scriptures. We must approach these questions with humility, openness, and acceptance, knowing that many—even among those who readily accept the sacramental approach of the means of grace—will not agree on every point. This is okay. God's grace is bigger than our differences.

---

[63]   Bromiley, 275–279.

[64]   See 1 Corinthians 11:17-34, and particularly the rendering of the KJV.

Questions for Reflection and Discussion

Chapter Three

♦ What is a sacrament?

♦ What is the difference, if any, between a general means of grace and a sacrament?

♦ What is the difference, if any, between a sacrament and a sacramental?

♦ What role does a response of faith play in receiving: (a) the means of grace; (b) the sacraments?

♦ What is an ordinance?

♦ What is the difference, if any, between a sacrament and an ordinance?

♦ In addition to Baptism and Holy Communion, do you believe that there may be other sacraments? If so, list and describe each.

♦ What role do the sacraments play in your spiritual life? Would you like to see this role increase or decrease? How might you accomplish either?

Through the Blessed Waters

Through the blessed waters, Lord
  and by your word we know
You give to us your love and life
  and in our hearts you show
How you would that we might live
  and to your world that we should give
The blessings of your Gospel Truth,
  and all your wonders show.

The power of your Spirit, Lord
  is present here today
Through simple Means of water now,
  within our hearts to stay
And as our faithful prayers do rise
  your grace now comes to change our lives
The glorious Majesty on high
  is present here to stay.

Baptismal waters now do pour,
  upon this soul of mine
They flow across this brow
  as a gracious, wondrous sign
That into Christ am I now plunged
  and all my sins are now expunged
Immersed, eternal, in God's love
  for all the world a sign.

So all remember here, today,
  the gift of water given
Baptismal graces now abound,
  eternally forgiven
Forever know the love of Christ
  never doubt or fear his life
And know, with faith and inward sight,
  your sins are all forgiven.

Gregory S. Neal †
November 19, 1997

Chapter Four

Baptism As a Means of Grace

W hat is baptism? Our brothers and sisters among the Baptist Churches, the Church of Christ and the Christian Church, as well as among several other Reformed communions, unequivocally assert that baptism is an ordinance. For them, it functions as the believer's affirmation of faith in Jesus Christ as Lord and Savior. Catholic Christians, inclusive of Anglicans, Methodists, Lutherans, many Presbyterians, and several other communions, all affirm that baptism is a sacrament. As such, Baptism functions as a means of grace through which Christians are initiated into the Body of Christ and given the grace they need to live by faith and grow in God's love. This chapter will consider these two approaches, and attempt to present an understanding of baptism as both a means of grace and a sacrament.

The *New Catechism* of the Roman Catholic Church offers the following short definition of the Sacrament of Baptism:

> Holy Baptism is the basis of the whole Christian life, the gateway to life in the Spirit ... and the door which gives access to the other sacraments. Through Baptism we are freed from sin and reborn as sons of God; we become members of Christ, are incorporated into the Church and made sharers in her mission: "Baptism is the sacrament of regeneration through water and the word."[65]

---

[65]   *The Catechism of the Catholic Church* (Liguori: Liguori Publications, 1994), 312.

Most catholic Christians will accept much or all of the above definition. Indeed, many Protestant baptismal doctrines contain remarkably similar ideas. One critical concept—baptism as a means of grace—can be seen clearly articulated in the statement: "Baptism is the sacrament of regeneration through water and the word." Baptism isn't just an outward act or ritual; it is a channel through which God's transforming love converts us.

This accords well with the definition of the sacraments outlined in the previous chapter. A sacrament is an outward and visible sign of an inward and spiritual grace to which we have the duty to respond. Initially, the grace that is received through the Sacrament of Baptism is identified as being prevenient in nature. It comes to us before any action of our own, working within us a miracle of spiritual awakening. Apart from the prevenient grace of God, we remain blind to our sins and ignorant of our need for forgiveness. But in God's gracious love, the death of Jesus on the cross for the sins of the whole world enables the spiritual sight of God's children. This inward and spiritual grace, given to all humankind, is recognized and proclaimed, symbolized and actualized through the outward and visible sign of the sacramental act of baptism.

Baptism is not just a profession of our faith. Relative to the faith of the Church in administering the sacrament it certainly is an act of faith—faith that Jesus Christ is present, bestowing divine favor. Far more importantly, however, baptism is an *instrument* of God's grace. It proclaims the universal love and presence of Jesus for and to all creation as well as to the specific child of God who receives the sacrament. It is a means of grace whereby we may know that God's love is sure and ready to save and transform us. As the Anglican-Methodist *Articles of Religion* affirm:

> Baptism is not only a sign of profession and mark of
> difference whereby Christians are distinguished from
> others that are not baptized; but it is also a sign of

regeneration or the new birth. The baptism of young children is to be retained in the church.[66]

The nature of baptism as an effective means of grace is thus affirmed, though in this version of the Article the instrumentality of the sacrament is not so clearly asserted. It should be noted that the original form of the article adds, after the semicolon, the following words:

> … whereby, as by an instrument, they that receive Baptism rightly are grafted into the Church; the promises of the forgiveness of sin, and of our adoption to be the sons of God by the Holy Ghost, are visibly signed and sealed; Faith is confirmed, and Grace increased by virtue of prayer unto God.[67]

Firstly, this historic doctrinal statement establishes that Holy Baptism is far more than just a symbolic act that Christians make when professing their faith; something is *actually* happening in the act, for it is "a sign of regeneration or the new birth." To use a bit of evangelical terminology, baptism is the normative sign of the "born-again experience;" in other words, all baptized and confirmed Christians have been "born from above."[68] Secondly, this article tells us that baptism is the normal means by which Christians are made part of the body of Christ. And, thirdly, the doctrine supports the continued practice of infant baptism.

All three of these points should make it clear that Holy Baptism is more than just an ordinance: something we do because we are told to do it. Rather, baptism is a sacrament: something that God does for us and to which we have the joy and calling to respond. We must

---

[66]   Article XVII, The Methodist Articles of Religion, *The Book of Discipline of The United Methodist Church, 2012.*

[67]   Article XXVII, The Anglican Articles of Religion, *The Book of Common Prayer.*

[68]   John 3:1–10

remember that, despite how it may look on the outside, God is always the primary actor in baptism. We are not the primary agency of action; we are the recipients of the action. We come to the sacrament because, through it, God's presence is made known and active in our lives. It is a means of grace through which Christians are made members of the Church Universal. They are also preveniently set upon the road to justification, sanctification, and perfection through the active power and presence of the Holy Spirit.

Succinctly, the Sacrament of Baptism should be understood as being:

- God's action, not ours.
- Not dependent upon our prior action.
- Always calling forth our response of faith.
- Not confined to the limited temporality of the baptismal ritual, but a lifelong process of grace and response.

This final point is *very* important for, as the linguistic examination will subsequently show, the Sacrament of Holy Baptism is *entirely* misunderstood if it is thought of as being an exclusively external ritual, temporally confined to the crude, physical, outward act of being baptized. Ontologically[69] speaking, baptism is the very beginning of the way of eternal life and our only mode of Christian existence.[70] This may seem like something of a radical affirmation, but this could be said of any sacrament and, indeed, of all the means of grace. God's grace is *that* important.

---

[69]   *Ontologically* means "of or relating to the most fundamental aspect of being."
[70]   See 1 Peter 3:31. We will return to this verse later.

Linguistic Considerations

"And baptism, which this prefigured, now saves you..."
– 1 Peter 3:21a

The fountain wasn't all that large, nor was it really very deep. In fact, it was about knee-deep at most, and there was a littering of coins strewn across the bottom: quarters, dimes, nickels, and a profusion of pennies, all tossed in by passers-by in hopes of "good luck." It might have been sufficiently deep for baptizing someone, were they willing to be plunged under the frigid waters on a cold, wet, late November day. At least, that must have been what crossed Gary's mind as he and I slowly walked through the park and past the fountain in its middle.

As usual, our conversation had ranged widely that day, spanning matters of Church history, systematic theology, and national politics, to the caustic personalities of the internet characters with whom we had frequently tangled on several online theological discussion boards. Earlier that day, we had spent several hours combing the shelves of a used bookstore, each seeking pearls of wisdom among the stacks of dusty, tired, mostly forgotten volumes. Gary had been in search of various specific commentaries on particular books of the Bible, while I had been seeking books on New Testament textual criticism, Christology and the theology of the sacraments. I had achieved some measure of success in my venture that day, coming across several works which had been on my list of "books to buy," including most especially the *coup* of the day: the classic masterpiece of Presbyterian Sacramental Theology: *Christic Baptism and Patristic Baptism* by James W. Dale.

Thanks to my good fortune at the bookstore, I had been in a buoyant, chatty, somewhat combative mood all day long. Our lunch, a fattening but wonderful plate of Kansas City BBQ from Arthur Bryant's, was carried forth with much sparring over matters both theological and political; and our conversation had spilled over into our afternoon of lazy exercise. Again, as was frequently the case and in part due to my purchase of the Dale text, the topic of our discussion had turned to baptism—a matter of some serious importance to Gary because, according to him, I had not been "really baptized."

I had been baptized in the Methodist Church by pouring, not by immersion, and, to add insult to injury, as an infant! Gary, being a minister in the Christian Church[71], which only practices believers' baptism by immersion, didn't consider my baptism valid. As a result, the state of my eternal soul had been on Gary's mind for several years. Don't misunderstand me: Gary professes me to be his brother in Christ, and while he and I have had our significant differences over the years, we can always affirm together that Jesus Christ, fully God and fully human, is our risen Lord and Savior. Nevertheless, the nagging question of my baptism, and what would happen to me if I died not having been immersed as a believer, had periodically plagued Gary.

That must have been what caused it. At least, I can't imagine why else he would have done such a thing, unless it was the frustration he might have been feeling over the fact that I had been particularly strident and combative during our debate over lunch.

At any rate, we had stopped by the fountain to survey the park and pick our course for the last leg of our journey, when Gary said: "You know, Greg, we could take care of your baptism right here, right now."

"How?" I asked, as I leaned over to tie a loose shoelace.

"The fountain." Gary gestured, "we could get in it and I could baptize you. Problem solved, case closed."

"Unnecessary."

"Oh?"

"Yep." I finished tying the loose shoelace, and proceeded to tighten the other as I said, "Because, you see, I've already been baptized. One Lord, one Faith ..."

---

[71]   A denomination which styles itself a "New Testament Church."

And, as I stood up straight, Gary reached out and—with the flat of his palm pressed firmly against my chest—he pushed me back over and into the fountain as he completed the affirmation: "...one Baptism."

That water was *cold.*

* * *

Gary is still one of my best friends. Fountains and all joking not withstanding, were I not already baptized I would have been pleased and honored to have Gary baptize me. He and I, like much of Christianity, simply have a difference of opinion on the issue of the nature and function of baptism; Gary operates from a strictly ordinance perspective. And, within ordinance theology, baptism is something that *we* do; being baptized is *our* proclamation of *our* faith in Jesus Christ as Lord and Savior. As such, the practice of, for example, infant baptism is in sharp contradiction to his interpretation of the purpose of the rite. The cognitive ability of the person being baptized is the principle issue here. It's not a matter of God's love for children—no, it's entirely the question of an infant's inability to make a profession of faith at the moment of their baptism.

Something very similar can be said concerning the mode of baptism. If baptism is an ordinance, something that we do rather than something that God does to us, then the *way* we are baptized takes on critical importance. It must be done by a believer in a form that reflects the supposed "Biblical" pattern. It must be a baptism into Christ's death, symbolized by going down into the water, followed by a resurrection to life eternal, symbolized by being brought up out of the water. Without being dipped into and removed from water, ordinance Christians do not consider the rite a valid baptism.

On both grounds—cognitive ability and mode of baptism—I failed to meet the ordinance paradigm. When I was three months old, during a regular Sunday morning worship service at Walnut Hill Methodist Church in Dallas, Texas, water was poured over my head and the Reverend Ira Galloway prayed, "Gregory Scott Neal, I baptize thee in the name of the Father, and of the Son, and of the Holy Spirit." For sacramental Christians this kind of baptism is not at all problematic. Indeed, in many churches it is quite common. For those who come from the ordinance perspective, however, infant baptism by pouring or sprinkling is quite invalid. And this is because of their particular understanding of the meaning of the Greek word for "baptism." They believe that baptism literally means to immerse or dip someone into water, and then bring them back up. Since baptism by pouring or sprinkling water doesn't in any way reflect what they believe to be the meaning of the word "baptism," they deny that such actions are *actually* baptisms at all. Unfortunately, their understanding of the meaning of the word "baptism" is quite incorrect, as a close study of the original Greek word demonstrates.

The Greek word βαπτιζω (*baptizo*) does not mean "to dip." It has never had that meaning and can *never* have it without a total change in its essential linguistic character. "To dip" properly translates the Greek word βαπτω (*bapto*), which is the temporary action of putting an item in water and then, almost immediately, bringing it back out.[72] When I wash my dinner dishes I run a sink full of soapy hot water and then, carefully dip each dish into the water, where I scrub it with a brush. As I finish cleaning off each dish, I transfer it to the right-hand sink where I spray it with cold water before placing it on the drip-dry rack. Each dish has been temporarily submerged into the water and then removed. They have not, however, been immersed; they have *not* been "baptized."

Βαπτιζω *(baptizo)* is governed by the temporal sense of permanence. It means "to immerse *and leave there*," which is radically different from "to dip and remove." To engage in *baptizo* is not to dip something temporarily into water and then remove it; it

---

[72]   Bauer, 132–133

is to submerge that something and *leave it there*.[73] The *Titanic* was baptized (i.e., sunk) in the North Atlantic.

Let me make sure that I am being completely understood here. "To immerse" is a permanent and all-encompassing action *without* a subsequent removal, while "to dip" involves putting-in and then taking-out. According to James W. Dale, in his classic: *Christic Baptism and Patristic Baptism*:

> "Dip" puts its object in a condition of intusposition momentarily; it puts in and draws out; βαπτιζω demands a condition of intusposition for its object without any limitations as to the time of continuance in such condition, but allows it to remain for ages or an eternity.[74]

Is baptism a temporary state or a permanent one? If baptism means to dip into Christ *and then remove,* then we have a serious theological problem on our hands; no one could be said to be "in Christ" except for that short period of time when they were under the baptismal waters. This is not correct. One is *permanently* immersed into Christ, never *temporarily* dipped into Jesus and then removed. We are baptized into an eternal relationship with Jesus, and that is the essential meaning here of the word βαπτιζω. The idea of Baptism *only* being a temporary dipping of a person into water coordinates neither with the linguistic meaning of *baptizo* nor with the theological essence of what it means to live eternally in the baptized life of Christ.

Ordinance Christians, and particularly Zwinglians, frequently make the argument that baptism is a burial into Christ's death and

---

[73]   ibid., 131–132. One of the given definitions in Bauer's lexicon is "to dip;" however the morphological root here is what is being appealed to, not the temporal character. Bauer is reflecting upon the ritual practice of immersion as one of the meanings of baptism. Linguistically speaking, however, baptism means to place within and leave there.

[74]   James W. Dale, *Christic Baptism and Patristic Baptism* (Wauconda: Bolchazy-Carducci Publishers, 1874/1994), 22.

a resurrection with Christ's glory. Theologically speaking, they are correct; that *is* what is going on in Christian baptism. However, their subsequent claim that only dipping someone into water actualizes their burial into Christ, and then that only their being brought out of the water can actualize their resurrection into God's glory is simply unsupported by either the Biblical witness or the linguistic meaning of the words used. Water cannot be directly related to our Lord's death, for Jesus was not executed by drowning nor was he buried at sea. I periodically like to taunt Gary, with my tongue planted firmly in my cheek, by asking him: "if this image of burial and resurrection is so important, why don't we baptize people by burying them in a tomb and then, three days later, exhuming them?"

What does Scripture have to say about baptism? Paul, in his letter to the Church in Rome, wrote:

> How can we who died to sin go on living in it? Do you not know that all of us who have been baptized into Christ Jesus were baptized into his death? Therefore we have been buried with him by baptism into death, so that, just as Christ was raised from the dead by the glory of the Father, so we too might walk in newness of life.[75]

This is the most important proof-text that many ordinance theologians, including my friend, Gary, use in support of their belief that baptism *must* be done by dipping (or, as they say, "immersing") an individual into water. This is claimed despite the fact that there is no mention of actually dipping someone into and out of water. There is not even any explicit mention of water in the passage. The idea that the ritual of baptism is referenced in this passage is not well conceived and is certainly not based upon anything that is in the passage itself. Those who have a preconception of how baptism should be performed

---

[75]   Romans 6:2b–4

read it into the passage; they look to this passage for scriptural language to support their belief. While the passage speaks about *real* baptism—baptism into the death and resurrection of Jesus—it does so without saying anything about *how* such a baptism occurs. The only way that one can conclude that the passage says something about *how* one should go about actually baptizing another is if one makes the Zwinglian assumption that baptism is nothing more than our profession of faith. For sacramental Christians this is entirely mistaken precisely because we look upon baptism as being a means of grace, an outward and visible sign of an inward and spiritual grace. It is an error of philosophical principle to give greater importance to the inferior external symbol rather than to the superior internal grace—that would be like preferring your reflection in the mirror to the reality of your actual face.

It is also impossible to convert the terms and symbolic imagery of this passage into liturgical practice. Firstly, to create the interpretation that is forced upon Romans 6:2-4 by the ordinance-Zwinglians,[76] one would have to rewrite it so that it would read something like this:

> As many of us as were dipped in water into Christ,
> were dipped in water into his death; Therefore we are
> buried with him by dipping in water into his death.[77]

This would allow us to interpret the passage as an institution of ritual baptism in the manner in which ordinance theologians claim it must be practiced. However, such a construction is impossible because:

- To substitute the meaning of βαπτω for the meaning of βαπτιζω would be to exchange a temporary act ("dipping") for a permanent act ("immersion"). Remember, immersion into Christ is a permanent state, not a temporary one. One is

---

76 Bromiley, 277.
77 Dale, 242.

not baptized into Christ and then withdrawn from him. One is baptized into Christ and left there.

- It destroys the theological meaning of the phrases "baptized into Christ" and "baptized into his death" by exchanging water for both Christ and his death. Jesus, not water, saves.
- Paul never wrote anything else even remotely similar to this.

Secondly, an ordinance-based reconstruction of this passage is impossible because baptism into water is *impossible*. If we were to immerse people into water, and then leave them there (for that is what it means to immerse something), we would be drowning them! Baptism into Christ Jesus, being immersed into our Lord and staying there, is the very *essence* of salvation and the whole point of Paul's argument. Ordinance theologians, in their desire to find a theological justification for their practice of baptism by plunging people into water and bringing them out, have misunderstood the essence of the nature of baptism. It's not about plunging someone into water and then bringing him or her out; it's about immersing one into Christ Jesus for all eternity.

To summarize, Baptism by "immersion" into water is a linguistic misnomer. *No* literal immersion occurs, even in Ordinance baptism, because to "immerse" someone means that he or she is placed into a different medium *and left there*. Since Ordinance Christians don't drown people in their baptisms, they are not really "immersing" them. In actuality, "dipping" the candidates temporarily into water is how they perform the ritual act of baptism.

This being said, it is nevertheless important for us to affirm that this form of ritual baptism *is* an outward and visible sign of the inward and spiritual grace of Baptism. Please do not misunderstand: baptism by dipping one in and out of water *is* a form of Christian baptism. However, its identity as baptism is *not* in any way dependent upon its mode of operation, because to dip under and bring up is *not* the linguistic meaning of the Greek word βαπτίζω. Again, *baptizo* means "to plunge something into a different medium *and leave it there.*" Be it performed by dipping into water and then bringing back out, or be it done by pouring or sprinkling water over the head of the one being baptized, *theologically* speaking Christian baptism *is* immersion into Christ Jesus. It is immersion into his death and into his eternal life through the power of the Holy Spirit. And it is our living in this baptismal life that saves us.

"But what about 1 Peter 3:21?" Good question! I opened the section on linguistic considerations with this quote because it applies rather well to the ordinance misunderstanding of the meaning of the word *baptizo*. The passage in question reads: "And baptism, which this prefigured, now saves you."[78] The word here is *not* the verb βαπτιζω. Instead of it being a verb, here it is the noun βαπτισμα. *Baptisma* is the very substance of divine life with Christ; it is the relationship, the state of being, the *nature* of living in Christ Jesus. In other words, it is the inward and spiritual grace that is related by the outward and visible sign of baptism with water. And this is precisely 1 Peter 3:21 is saying: living in the baptismal relationship, within the body of Christ (as Noah and his family lived together in the Ark), saves us. Living in the grace and life of our Lord and Savior, Jesus Christ, is what saves us. Baptism is not the act of being washed in the water, but rather it is the *state* of immersion into Christ. And, this immersion is true, and certain, regardless of the mode of the outward and visible sign. The Church, as God's agency in the world, proclaims the actualizing words "I baptize thee in the name of the Father, and of the Son, and of the Holy Spirit." It is God who baptizes through the power of the Holy Spirit.

---

[78]   1 Peter 3:21

Infant Baptism

> "Truly I tell you, unless you change and become like children,
> you will never enter the kingdom of heaven. Whoever becomes
> humble like this child is the greatest in the kingdom of heaven.
> Whoever welcomes one such child in my name welcomes me."
> —*Matthew 18:3-5*

"Upon what grounds do you baptize infants?" Even those who understand and accept that baptism is a means of grace, a sacrament and not an ordinance, sometimes have a problem with the idea of a baby being a fit candidate for baptism. Those who have this problem see the Christian's response of faith as being of critical importance in bringing the sacrament to fruition, and the fact that infants cannot immediately profess their faith in Jesus Christ is a serious problem. Since babies can't make a profession of faith at the time of their baptism, they shouldn't be baptized. Remarks like these have crept up, from time to time, in my congregations both in Texas and in North Carolina, causing me to chuckle; it would appear that there is a little bit of an Anabaptist hanging around in some United Methodists!

Another objection I have sometimes heard is that "a child can't understand what's going on when they're being baptized, hence we should wait until they're old enough to understand." This remark is usually well-responded to by asking the simple question: "what, precisely, is going on when an *adult* is baptized?" The assumption being made is that comprehension and informed consent are of critical importance in the sacrament, an idea that misses the whole point of a sacrament as a means of grace. Sacraments are God's doing, not ours. Our ability or inability to comprehend the sacrament in no way limits God's ability to move in our lives. How many adults *truly* comprehend, at the time of their baptism, what's going on in the sacrament? If believers can be unclear as to what baptism is all about—other than having some vague notion that it is a rite of initiation (which is, frequently, how it is initially understood)—then why worry about waiting for children to gain greater understanding? If comprehension is so important, why not require all adults to wait until they have developed an in-depth understanding of the theological and biblical intricacies of sacramental theology?

All of this raises an important question concerning an idea that is at the heart of the Campbellite (Church of Christ) movement, as well as being a principle issue in Zwingli's theology. Essentially, most ordinance theologians—be they Zwinglians, Campbellites, Baptists, or some other brand—tend to assert that "what Scripture does not command, the Church is forbidden to practice." The idea here is that the scriptures are so central to the Christian life that everything we do as the people of God should be articulated and carried forth from within the context of scriptural warrants. Put another way, scripture is understood as setting limits for both the inner boundaries—what one must believe in order to be saved—and the outer boundaries—what one is free to do and believe. Zwingli, for his own part and to his own credit, always tried to present Biblical arguments for all of his positions. Whether or not he succeeded in this endeavor is another matter. Indeed, it is very doubtful that any Christian, even the strictest Church of Christ Campbellite, has ever managed to establish an expression of the faith and a way of life that is in *total* accord with a pattern derived *solely* from scripture. Regardless of how much one would like to conceive of themselves as being a "New Testament Christian," the simple fact remains that *everyone* functions as if what the scripture does not forbid us to do or believe, the Church is free to exercise. While most Christians will affirm that the Scriptures provide an inner boundary concerning what *must* be believed for salvation, very few Christians actually believe—and *none* actually practice—the ideal of the outer boundary. All Christians, *without exception,* believe and practice things that are not authorized by Scripture. Campbellites might not like to admit it, but this is as true for them as it is for Methodists, Lutherans, and Roman Catholics. All Christians *behave* as if the Scriptures do not place an outward limit on what may be believed; so long as the Bible does not prohibit it, it may be believed or practiced.

This is the official position of most Protestant denominations. The Anglican-Methodist Articles of religion articulate this idea with a clarity that is both rare and refreshing:

> The Holy Scriptures containeth all things necessary to salvation; so that whatsoever is not read therein, nor may be proved thereby, is not to be required of any man that it should be believed as an article of faith, or be thought requisite or necessary to salvation.[79]

This doctrinal position should make it clear that, even for Protestant catholics, the Bible is indeed central to Christian life and faith. The Bible is authoritative because it is the norm by which the requirements for salvation are established. If a theological opinion or belief is not found in the scriptures, or if it otherwise cannot be supported through a careful study of the scriptures, than it *cannot* be required that a person believe it.[80]

The Scriptures are thusly understood as setting the inner limits of Christian faith, on those things that must be believed. On matters where they are silent, Christians are free to have a multitude of opinions. Unless one is willing to throw away all Church buildings and cease the use of all electronic devices for communicating the Gospel, etc., and return to the confines of New Testament-era practices, this is the principle which should be adopted.

The polarization of these two positions, and the uncritical and inconsistent ways in which the Sacramental and Ordinance sides of the debate apply them, has had unfortunate consequences for the development of Christian doctrine. Both need to honestly face the fact that, on the issue of infant baptism the New Testament is of less help

---

[79]   Article V, The Methodist Articles of Religion, *The Book of Discipline of The United Methodist Church, 2012*; Article VI, The Anglican Articles of Religion, *The Book of Common Prayer.*
[80]   For more on the subject of the authority of the scriptures, see chapter eight.

than we might wish. The Scriptures clearly do not prohibit the baptism of infants, and thus there is no scriptural rationale for denying the sacrament to babies. The only rationale for denying baptism to such *must* be located within an ordinance-based theological interpretation of baptism.

As has already been indicated, the Zwinglian approach to baptism is to view the rite as the Christian's profession of faith. It is an ordinance, something that we do, not a means of grace, which is something that God does. Surprisingly, while the early Zwingli denied that infants could be fit subjects for Christian baptism, in his later writings the Swiss reformer actually backtracked and identified, in the Old Testament type of circumcision, a warrant for infant baptism![81] Hence, at this point the Anabaptists and other ordinance theologians break with Zwingli. In their theological formulation, babies and young children are not fit subjects for Christian baptism because they can neither physically nor cognitively profess their faith in Jesus Christ as Lord and Savior. In other words, the strict ordinance approach affirms "Believers' Baptism." And, as such, it is very definitely understood as something that *we* do.

What Protestant catholics and Roman Catholics say regarding the baptism of infants can be summed up in a few short sentences. The baptism of infants proclaims, quite dramatically and most fully, what is still readily present and true relative to *all* baptisms, including those of adults: God, not the recipient, is the primary actor. If God is the actor, then any and all objections to infant baptism based upon a lack of cognition and an inability to profess one's faith are automatically invalidated. Indeed, infant baptism is as real as baptism gets. It is a far more striking illustration of the reality of our receptiveness in the sacrament than is adult baptism. An infant cannot make a decision to be baptized, nor can an infant immediately affirm his or her faith in Jesus. As such, an infant's baptism cannot be misinterpreted as a believers' baptism.

---

[81]   Bromiley, 278.

An adult's baptism holds both God's action and our response together at the same moment in time; an adult is baptized and then immediately makes his or her affirmation of faith. An infant's baptism separates the means of grace from the affirmation. A necessary separation of many years (often twelve or more) is imposed between God's action and the human response until the child is old enough to confirm his or her baptism. In an ontological sense, both forms of baptism are identical; both are acts of God, and both require a human response of faith.

From the divine perspective, there is no fundamental difference between an adult baptism and an infant baptism. In both, God acts and humans receive and respond. From the human perspective, however, the baptism of an adult believer more completely reveals the totality of baptism as a completed sacrament—God's act of imparting grace and our human response of faith. The human response is commonly referred to as *confirmation*, for the grace that God imparts to us is confirmed by our response of faith. In a believer's baptism, both God's act and our response occur at one moment in history.

In an infant baptism, however, the sacrament occurs across two different moments in history: one is baptized and then, at a later point in time (following years of cognitive development and preparation) the child/young adult proclaims his or her faith. Until confirmation, however, baptism is not a "completed" act. God's part is done, is sure, and is true. Our response is contingent; until we make our response by professing our faith in Jesus Christ, by making our confirmation, the Sacrament of Baptism is not "completed."

The problem, however, is only a problem in so far as human dependence upon temporality is concerned. For some reason we seem to think that it matters that a gulf of years separates an infant's baptism from her confirmation. For God, this is not an issue because time is not a limiting factor for the divine. Be it twelve seconds or twelve years, time is irrelevant with God; God acts and we respond.

Since baptism is understood as God's action, the age of the recipient—adult or infant—is not relevant. If the recipient is an adult, the ability to respond in faith is assumed, and *required*, for the baptism to be completed. If it's an infant, the ability to respond in faith is also assumed, and *required*, for the baptism to be completed. The *only* difference (from the human point of view) is that an adult can immediately confirm their baptism, while an infant must first grow old enough to make such a proclamation of faith. But, since it is God who is the principle actor in all baptisms, and not human beings, this is not a problem. It certainly hasn't been a problem for the vast majority of Christians throughout the greater portion of the history of the Church.

Indeed, the exclusion of infants from baptism is a relatively recent development, dating to the Anabaptists in Germany and the English Separatists (a.k.a. "Baptists") of the Reformation. References to infant baptism abound in the writings of the early church fathers. Possible references to infants being baptized can even be found in scripture (e.g. Acts 16:15 and 1 Corinthians 1:16). Such arguments, apart from further historical evidences, have never been *totally* convincing to me. The argument in favor of infant baptism from early Church practices can be strongly made, however.

St. Augustine, the influential fifth century theologian and Bishop of Hippo in North Africa, stated the belief and practice of his church on the subject of infant baptism:

> The infants are brought to church, and if they cannot go there on their own feet, they run with the feet of others ... Let no one among you, therefore, murmur strange doctrines. This the Church has always had, and this she has always held; this she received from the faith of the ancients; this she preserves tenaciously to the end.[82]

---

[82] Philip Schaff, ed., *Nicene and Post-Nicene Fathers, First and Second Series.* 28 Vols. (Peabody MA: Hendrickson Publishers, Inc., 1995), Augustine Sermon 176.

Augustine clearly affirms that infants are to be baptized; even young babies, who have to be carried to the church, should be brought in for baptism. This statement is of particular significance because it clearly demonstrates that not only was infant baptism being practiced in the church during Augustine's time, but also that it wasn't a recent innovation. Indeed, according to the bishop's own knowledge, considerable antiquity and ecclesiastical authority supported its practice. As Augustine said, "this the Church has always had, and this she has always held." In other words, infant baptism wasn't a new idea that he was putting forward; it was an *ancient* and well-established practice in the life of the Church.

And, indeed, in support of Augustine we have even older affirmations of the practice that can be found in the writings of the Church Fathers. For instance, St. Cyprian, addressing his fellow bishops at the Council of Carthage in 253 A.D., said to Fidus concerning the withholding of baptism to young children:

> No one agrees with you in your opinion as to what
> should be done, but we all, on the contrary, judge that
> to no one born of man was the mercy and the grace
> of God to be denied.[83]

The grace of God is affirmed as being available to all; it is to be denied to no one, regardless of age or cognitive ability. And, as Augustine's own commentary on Cyprian's remark indicates, this includes, most especially, infants:

> The Blessed Cyprian, not forming any new decree,
> but maintaining the assured faith of the Church, in
> order to correct those who held that an infant should
> not be baptized before the eighth day, gives it as his

---

[83]   Alexander Roberts and James Donaldson, eds., *Ante-Nicene Fathers.* 10 Vols. (Peabody MA: Hendrickson Publishers, Inc., 1995), vol. 5, Cyprian.

own judgment and that of his fellow bishops, that a
child can be validly baptized as soon as born."[84]

Attempts to restrict infant baptisms have occurred at various times
throughout the history of the Church; they are not unique to the
Anabaptists and the Reformation period. Nevertheless, denying
the sacrament to newborn babies was not common prior to the
Reformation; indeed, doing so was considered schismatic. Not even
an avoidable delay of eight days was considered reasonable. Babies
were to be baptized at the earliest opportunity.

In the eastern Church, at about the same time as Cyprian, the
famous third century Christian scholar Origen said: "The Church
hath received it as a tradition from the Apostles that infants, too,
ought to be baptized."[85] And, long before either Cyprian or Origen,
St. Irenaeus, the second century Bishop of Lyons in southern France,
wrote:

> Christ came to save all through Himself – all, I say,
> who through Him are born again in God: infants and
> little children and boys and young men and old men.[86]

This affirmation of infant baptism, and of its nature as a means
of grace *even* for "infants and little children," comes from around
the year 140 A.D. It highlights the great antiquity of the practice of
infant baptism, and the fact that such early Christians didn't view
the practice as being in any way different from the baptism of adults.
Quite the contrary; for Irenaeus even babies and little children were
considered "born again in God" through baptism. This is a powerful
statement, and one which will give both evangelicals and mainline
Protestants at least some trouble. Nevertheless, if understood from
within the whole context of what a sacrament actually is—a means

---

[84]   Schaff, vol. 4, *Augustine*.
[85]   Roberts, vol. 4, *Origen*.
[86]   ibid. vol. 1, *Irenaeus*.

of grace, to which we must respond before it is complete—then the objections that even I may have to Irenaeus' affirmation drop away.

Some of the best archeological evidence concerning the antiquity of infant baptism can be found in the Roman catacombs. Two inscriptions, among several similar examples, are of particular note. In the first one, a late first-century Christian named Murtius Verinus placed on the tomb of his children the inscription: "Verina received baptism at the age of ten months, Florina at the age of twelve months." The date of this tomb has been established as being around the year 110 A.D. Another tomb, not far away from this one, has the inscription: "Here rests Achillia, a newly-baptized infant; she was one year and five months old, died February 23rd...." and then follows the year of the reigning emperor, which dates her death to 91 A.D.[87]

Such archeological evidence, when combined with the writings of so many Church Fathers from as far back as Irenaeus in the mid-second century A.D., demonstrates that the practice of infant baptism has been known and accepted in the Church from the time of the apostles. Since infant baptism is so well attested throughout the history of the Church, its practice can be seen as undergirding our understanding of the nature of the sacraments in general, and of baptism in particular. Baptism is not something that we do; fundamentally speaking it is something that God does to, for, and within us.

Since the scriptures do not forbid infant baptism, and since the sacramental understanding of baptism does not recognize a distinction between adult and infant baptism, and since the traditions of the early church and the archeological evidence show clear signs of the practice of infant baptism as early as 91 A.D., in my opinion there is no convincing argument against infant baptism. In the very least, it must be recognized that infant baptism is just as valid, just as *real* a baptism as that of an adult.

Why, then, do so many Christians—indeed, many sacramental Christians—persist in thinking that there is a difference between

---

[87]   W. Wall, *History of Infant Baptism, 2 Vols.* (London, 1900), 37–114.

infant and adult baptism? This persistence can be seen manifested in many different ways. For example, in my pastorates I periodically have people say to me things like, "I was christened as a baby, but now that I'm an adult and know what I'm doing I want to be *really* baptized." My response is to ask them to consider the question of God's grace in the sacrament. "Is God's grace a failure because you, as a child, couldn't respond at the time with faith?"

In such cases, I like to offer people who are seeking re-baptism the option of reaffirming their baptisms in a ritual that even includes the sprinkling of water upon them and upon the whole congregation. This is *not*, in *any* way, to be thought of as being a re-baptism. I do not pronounce, "I baptize you in the name of the Father, and of the Son, and of the Holy Spirit" when I sprinkle them and/or the congregation with water. No, this is a *reaffirmation* of one's baptism, a time and a way to become reconnected with the grace that began one's Christian journey. This has almost always been sufficient for those who really just want to re-live the baptismal experience; it also satisfies their desire to make a public affirmation of faith in direct relation to their baptisms. Indeed, this is something that I offer to all those who come for confirmation. It enables a meaningful reconnection with their baptism, regardless of the interval involved.

Another way in which some Christians will try to understand infant baptism as being something less than *real* baptism is through their terminology. In the request that I quoted above, the individual asserted that they had been "christened" before, but now they wanted to be baptized. Christening is a term that is used, in some Churches, for the baptism of infants. However, it is my impression that it does more to confuse matters than it does to help them. Indeed, I find the term itself to be absolutely fascinating because "christening" is what we do to a ship when we break a bottle of champagne on its prow and both name and officially launch it. When I hear the term "christening," I cannot help but imagine a minister breaking a bottle of champagne over the head of a baby—hardly a holy sight!

We don't "christen;" we sprinkle or pour water over an infant's head, baptizing the child in the name of the Father, and of the Son, and of the Holy Spirit. While christening may be thought of as the part of the baptismal liturgy in which the child receives her Christian name, it is not an alternate term for infant baptism. Baptism is baptism regardless of the age or cognitive abilities of the recipient. Do any who speak of infant baptism as a "christening" also call an adult baptism a "christening?" I seriously doubt if the thought of doing so has ever entered their minds. And, these Protestants do this because they tend to look upon infant baptism as being something other than *real* baptism. And, in this they are mistaken.

Confirmation

> For one believes with the heart and so is justified,
> and one confesses with the mouth and so is saved.
> —*Romans 10:10-13*

Protestant catholics affirm that baptism is a sacrament, not an ordinance. It is an act of God. This, however, doesn't mean that we don't have a response to make. To the contrary, we have the responsibility of responding to God's gift of grace with faith; in other words, we should "confirm" our baptisms by professing our faith in Jesus Christ as Lord and Savior. Indeed, an affirmation of our faith is required before our baptisms are "complete." The sacrament is God's act, but it is incomplete until we respond.

Within the Roman Catholic Church, Confirmation is viewed as a separate sacrament. Within Protestant catholic circles it is sometimes viewed as being a part of the Sacrament of Baptism. This may well be one of the reasons why the rite is found in the United Methodist baptismal liturgy.[88] It would appear that United Methodists, like

---

[88]   *UM Hymnal*, 37.

many Protestants, understand Confirmation as the completion of Holy Baptism: you cannot have one without having the other. This holds true for adults, who can confirm God's grace at the time of their baptisms, as well as for infants who must wait for a period of years before they may be confirmed.

But what does Confirmation do? It is our affirmation of faith, our response to grace, our saying "yes" to God's love. In confirmation, the baptized are saying, for the first time before a congregation, that they claim for themselves the grace which was proclaimed for them in their baptisms. Confirmation, hence, completes the Sacrament of Baptism. For those who are baptized as infants, the response of faith in confirmation cannot come until the child attains the mental and emotional maturity to be able to affirm that God's grace has moved them to faith in Jesus Christ as Lord and Savior. For those who are baptized as either youth or adults, confirmation may well occur immediately after the application of the baptismal waters.

This should illustrate that what is going on in the baptism of an infant is *identical* to what is going on in the baptism of a "believer." *Both* reflect God's grace, which comes before anything we do. Baptism may be understood as reflecting prevenient grace; Confirmation can be understood as reflecting justifying grace. In Confirmation, the believer affirms their faith in Jesus Christ and enters into full membership within the Body of Christ. In the Sacrament of Baptism, God claims us as his very own children; in Confirmation *we* proclaim God as our Eternal Father, and Jesus Christ as our Lord and Savior.

Questions for Reflection and Discussion

Chapter Four

♦   What is the meaning of the word "baptism?"

♦   What does it mean, theologically, for one to be baptized?

♦   Who is the primary actor in baptism?

♦   Do you remember your own baptism? If so, describe it.

♦   If you cannot remember your own baptism, describe the first time that you ever saw a baptism. What did you think was going on?

♦   If you have gone through confirmation or first public affirmation of faith, describe what that was like.

♦   Do you feel your confirmation, or first public affirmation of faith, still has meaning in your life today? Sometimes people feel that they should repeat their affirmation of faith again; would you like to do so?

♦   Have you ever experienced a worship service in which you were invited to remember your baptism?

Holy Presence

Come with open, contrite hearts to this Holy Table, set
       Before us by our Loving Lord,
       The Means of Grace to afford,
And hungry hearts to bless.

"I am the bread of life," said He, and so we come, yet
       Wondering upon this Holy Mystery,
       Proclaimed for all eternity,
In simple means before us set.

"This is my Body ... This is my Blood," the Holy One did say
       To us that night, so long ago
       When God's loving Grace did flow,
Into our hungry hearts to stay.

His Holy Presence here is Real, though how this is we cannot say
       'Tis only ours to be made ready,
       To come with faithful hearts made steady,
And eat and drink and pray.

The Grace of Christ is offered here, in all its mystery,
       Through simple, Holy Bread and Wine,
       With upturned eyes and open mind,
We receive God's Power Divine.

So eat, dear friends, the offered gifts of Holy sustenance,
       Celebrate this mighty feast,
       Let every sinful thought now cease,
And go forth now in Peace.

Gregory S. Neal †
August 1995

Chapter Five

Holy Communion As a Means of Grace

T he focused efforts of study, research, and intense spiritual inquiry which went into my graduate theological education at Duke Divinity School were exhilarating for me. Physically, mentally, emotionally and spiritually, I was pushed and pulled, prodded and expanded, *far* beyond the limits of my wildest imagination. They were years of deep personal growth and were both wonderful *and* trying for me. Staying up *late* into the night—and, frequently, all night long—reading and writing, researching and studying, memorizing paradigms and conjugating verbs, arguing and debating, thinking and articulating concepts, all taxed me to the very limit of my endurance.

The amazing depth and diversity of advanced intellectual disciplines which the clergy are required to master *en route* to their ordinations sometimes goes unnoticed among those who have not had the experience of jumping through the hoops of a Board of Ordained Ministry. To put it simply, it's not an easy row to hoe. I know that some ministers miraculously managed to breeze through their seminary or graduate school years with little, if any, intellectual pressure or spiritual growth. They did what was required, but very little more. They produced adequate work, passed all the exams and wrote all the papers but only infrequently generated outstanding or original work.

Now, granted, not every pastor is, or even should be, an intellectual powerhouse; there is *substantially more* to ministry than being able to expound upon the intricacies of Systematic Theology, Church History, or the conjugation of Greek verbs. Some of the best clergy I know—some of the most *effective* ministers of the Gospel of Jesus Christ—are among those for whom Seminary and academic studies were either extremely difficult or of very little interest. However, striking a balance between mind and spirit *is* the objective of the graduate seminary, and sometimes even the most careful student can lose that balance. I speak from personal experience, having myself frequently gone off the deep end of academic pursuits. Others, like me, excelled in academia, but rarely allowed the experience of theological education and spiritual formation to affect them in an internal, emotional, personal way.

I can remember watching as a good friend and fellow student waltzed his way through a heart-wrenching program of Clinical Pastoral Education, oblivious to all the pain and anguish. As he put it, "I don't need to learn anything new about myself; I just want to teach. All these feelings will just get in the way." This attitude saddened me because I knew that this fellow would miss out on so much that would help him to understand and aid his future students. And it frightened me, because I knew that I was quite a bit like him. Had a special mentor, professor, and friend not guided me with much wise advice and counsel, I might have had the same attitude and experience. As it was, the studies and the emotional growth were difficult, painful, and frequently draining of physical and spiritual energy. I lost many months of sleep on lengthy religious debates with fellow students and in all-night study sessions that often seemed to go nowhere. In truth, I immensely enjoyed my years of graduate education and look back upon them with an idealized longing as one of the most exciting times of my life.

Of course, one might say that it was my own fault that my seminary experience was so exhausting. I didn't *have* to study Latin, Greek and Hebrew, nor did I have to take all those upper-level Ph.D. courses while still in the Master's program. But I thought that if I was going to be studying at one of the premier theological institutions on the planet, I should at least take advantage of it. And so I knocked myself out physically, intellectually, emotionally and spiritually.

In the midst of my studies I realized that I needed to do something to keep myself healthy, so every week I would escape the campus of Duke University and travel across the town of Durham, North Carolina, to a monastery of the Society of Saint John the Evangelist. St. John's House was a beautiful, wood-frame, one hundred-plus year-old, three-story manor surrounded by a lovely, sculpted, well-manicured yard and garden. It was the *perfect* place to lose oneself when the pressures of study, life, and spiritual formation grew too burdensome. Along with a number of other ministerial students from Duke Divinity, I went there each and every Saturday morning to worship, receive Holy Communion, and become re-energized for yet another week of academic excellence in the classroom, and a weekend of ministerial excellence in my student pastorate.

Throughout the week, amid the rigors of study and self-discovery, I would find myself looking forward to those Saturday morning worship services. Even despite the fact that I could and did worship every day at the Divinity School, where I received the Eucharist in York Chapel, I increasingly discovered that I craved the liturgy, thirsted for the Word, anticipated the holy silence, and longed after the Blessed Sacrament. It was as if I had become addicted to the means of grace which that wonderful monastic community made available to me. The monks, and their religious devotion, became the fuel for my spirit in a deserted land. Without these Saturday mornings, and the grace and peace of our Lord's real presence that they furnished me, I don't think I would have emotionally or spiritually survived.

I can remember stepping through the door of St. John's House on a misty, overcast, chilly Saturday morning, my mind filled with clutter and my spirit ill at ease, only to be met by the warm embrace, the love and acceptance, of one of the monks of this special community. Brothers Paul, Gross, Eldridge, David, Bob, Brian … it mattered not; they were all so *very* welcoming to my fellow seminarians and to me as we sought the presence of Jesus. It was like leaving behind the weights of the world, the pressures of existence, the fears and anxieties of life, the stresses and strains of academic endeavors, and entering the bliss of heaven.

I came, week after week, in search of God's grace; and I found it. I found it in a community of monks, in their love and service, in the Holy Scriptures, and above all in the Blessed Sacrament of Holy Communion—all of which they celebrated daily and of which we were warmly invited to partake. The bread and wine, the Word and the community, the prayers and the blessings ... these means of grace quickly became the fuel for my spiritual and intellectual life. Indeed, they became so important for me that even to this day, if a week goes by in which I do not receive the Eucharist and worship within a community of faith, I feel empty ... empty and in need of the inner presence of my Savior. This is what the many means of grace—and especially the sacrament of Holy Communion—do in my life.

The Blessed Sacrament makes known to us, through simple elements of bread and wine, the abiding love and life-transforming real presence of Jesus Christ. Holy Communion is the wonderful gift of the very life of God, which empowers us for Christian love and service. One of my seminary professors, Dr. Harmon Smith, used to say that the Eucharist is "the most significant moral act of the Church." By this, we took him to mean that through the Blessed Sacrament not only are we all united together as one body in Christ Jesus, but also that the moral and spiritual center of the Christian life depends upon the grace which comes to us through feasting at the Lord's Supper. I believe this professor to have been correct. Through the Blessed Sacrament of Holy Communion the Body of Christ is both established and empowered for service in and to God's world; through this holy meal of mystery we receive our unity, our calling, and the strength that we need to carry the Gospel of Jesus Christ to all people. If this isn't the root and identity of Christian spirituality and ethics, I don't know what else might qualify.

The Principle Question

> When he was at the table with them, he took bread, blessed and
> broke it, and gave it to them. Then their eyes were opened, and
> they recognized him; and he vanished from their sight.
> —*Luke 24: 30-31*

Holy Communion … the Eucharist … the Lord's Supper … the terms that we use for the Holy Meal all reflect its character as a means of grace. Take a moment to think about each term. When we speak of the Sacrament as being "Holy Communion," what we are doing is highlighting the unity that we receive through it. When we eat and drink of the elements, we are brought into a "holy communication" with God and are made one with each other in the Body of Christ. When we use the term "Eucharist," we highlight the powerful joy and the spirit of thanksgiving that we receive through the transforming grace of our savior. When we receive the Eucharist, we celebrate the feast of joy and offer our sacrifices of praise and thanksgiving for the gift of the real presence of Jesus in our lives. And, finally, when we use the term "the Lord's Supper," we lift the truth that this Holy Meal is really God's gift to us. It is *his* meal, not ours; we are honored to be invited to receive it along with all of his disciples. Just as Jesus blessed and broke the bread in Emmaus and Cleopas and the other disciple's eyes were opened to his real presence, so also today we are invited to his meal to have our eyes opened to Christ's real presence in our own lives. It truly is "the Supper of the Lord," for in it we receive Jesus as our source of eternal, sanctifying nourishment.

Through these three common terms, we can see and know the meaning of the sacrament and its nature as a means of grace for the life of the Church. And that is our principle question in this chapter: how is the real presence of Jesus communicated to us through this means of grace, and what does this wonderful gift mean for us?

Frequently it is said that there are many different ways to understand the meaning and function of the Lord's Supper. This is both true and false. It is true in that there are many different ways to think and talk about the Eucharist. It is false in that these many different ways can all be reduced to two fundamental approaches. We will begin with the approach that is popular among those who reject the very means of grace/sacramental concept that this book is all about, and then we will proceed to the approaches of Sacramental Christianity.

Memorial Representation

"This is my body, which is given for you. Do this in remembrance of me."
—*Luke 22:19b*

Zwingli was the first to understand Communion as being nothing more than a memorial meal. It is the point of view held by the Baptists, the Church of Christ, and many other related or similar denominations and independent ecclesial groups. Some see the meal as simply a reminder of the Last Supper, and hence there is *nothing* at all going on in the act that isn't understood to be happening *apart* from the act. This idea is sometimes called the doctrine of the "real absence" of Christ, and as such it reflects a radical point of view that even Zwingli himself would not have appreciated.

Others see the ordinance as having at least some degree of sacramental character, although instrumentality is still totally rejected. The Church, as it gathers around the table in faith, is understood as receiving divine grace *directly* from God, and not through the instrumentality of the elements of bread and wine. Essentially, the table has become irrelevant; the elements could be exchanged for pizza and beer or coffee and donuts, and God's grace could still be discerned as descending upon the gathered people of God.

Memorial Representation places the focus upon the believer and the believer's response of faith rather than upon God as the giver of divine grace. God is not thought of as being an actor in the ordinance *at all;* we are the actors in the Lord's Supper, eating and drinking the bread and wine as we remember Jesus. This is the cardinal difference between the sacramental and ordinance approaches to the means of grace in general, and to Holy Communion in particular. While the sacramental approach views the means as having an instrumental nature, the ordinance approach rejects the instrumental concept and focuses upon the role of the human in performing or "acting out" each of the means. Rather than being the means by which we receive God's grace, they become the means by which we express our faith. While the expression of one's faith *is* both an outgrowth and a form of the grace we receive, the ordinance approach robs the means of their essential role as the instrumental conveyers of Divine favor. And yet, this is the approach of Zwingli and the "iconoclastic reformers" of the Reformation.[89]

Zwingli's objection to a means of grace understanding of the Lord's Supper is rooted in his theological objection to the idea that created matter could cause or convey divine attributes. Indeed,

> Zwingli was reluctant to acknowledge any other causality than that of God, the first cause. Hence, the very notion of *sacramental* causality was offensive to him.[90]

For Zwingli, it was a fundamental flaw in reasoning to assign to created matter attributes that only divine matter could contain. Spiritual things could not be mastered, contained, or controlled by physical things. To localize the divine within a physical substance was to limit or attempt to control the divine, and for Zwingli that was heretical. Hence, he opposed the means of grace concept at its ontological core. For Zwingli, grace comes to the believer directly, and *only* directly, from God. The means do not cause, nor do they

---

[89]   Brown, 322–325.
[90]   Gerrish, 164.

convey or in any way mediate God's grace, although they *do* help to remind us of God's promise. The means do not empower or enable our faith, although through their symbolic character they *do* help to reinforce our faith.

According to Zwingli, the sacramental approach to the Lord's Supper fails to make the proper distinction between divine and human nature. Divine nature is ubiquitous—God is everywhere— while human nature is limited and cannot be everywhere. This was true for Jesus in his life on earth and, indeed, is still true for Jesus today in glory. While Zwingli admitted that Jesus, by virtue of his divinity, could easily be understood as being spiritually or symbolically, present in the sacrament, he denied that Jesus could be really, actually, or *bodily* present in the bread and wine of Holy Communion. Why? Because Jesus' body is in heaven, seated at the right hand of the Father. Being a human body, it could only be in one place at one time. Hence, since the body of Jesus is in heaven, at the right hand of the Father, it cannot *also* be in the elements of bread and wine on millions of altars throughout all space and time. Jesus *can* be said to be spiritually or symbolically present, but not *really* or *bodily* present. As Zwingli himself said:

> Omnipresence can pertain to the deity alone and may
> in no way be communicated to the human nature.
> His body after the resurrection cannot in any way
> be ubiquitous like the deity; according to the divine
> nature, he is everywhere.[91]

Hence, when Jesus says in the context of the Last Supper, "this is my body,"[92] Zwingli and the other ordinance theologians will argue that he did not mean it literally—the "is" should be taken as meaning "signifies" rather than as asserting the identity which is proclaimed.

---

[91]   Ulrich Zwingli, *Werk*, in *Corpus Reformatorum*, Karl G. Bretschneider and Heinrich E. Bindell, eds. (Peipzig: M. Heinsius, 1834ff), VIII, 639.

[92]   Matthew 26:26; Mark 14:22; Luke 22:19; 1 Corinthians 11:24

To rephrase Jesus in Zwinglian terms: "This *signifies* my body," not, "This *is* my body."

At first glance, this does appear to make a certain amount of sense. After all, during the Lord's Supper the flesh was still on Jesus' bones and the blood was still in Jesus' veins. If his body and blood were intact, how could bread and wine also be said to be his actual body and blood? Likewise, now his bodily presence is in heaven, at the right hand of the Father, and hence by its very human nature it cannot also be in Holy Communion. For Zwinglians, the bread and wine can be said to "signify" the real presence of Jesus, but neither can be said to actually *be*, contain, or convey the real presence of Jesus.

One of the strongest critiques of Zwingli's argument against the doctrine of Real Presence can be seen precisely at its christological foundation. While Zwingli accepted the Nicene profession of Jesus as being fully human and fully divine, when it came to the controversy over the Eucharist his desire to deny sacramental presence required him to accept incipient Nestorianism. Essentially, Zwingli's approach forces a division between the divine and the human natures of Jesus, something which is a no-no when it comes to orthodox Christology.

> ...with Zwingli there is [the threat] of Nestorianism, in
> which the two natures fall apart from one another...[93]

At first this might seem like a minor problem, but it is not; if followed to its logical conclusion, it can be a very serious theological error. To claim that Jesus is spiritually present, but cannot be physically or *really* present, is dangerous for it assumes that Jesus does some things as God but not as a human being, and other things as a human being but not as God.[94] This division is the very essence of Nestorianism.

---

[93]   Brown, 325.
[94]   I understand that John Wesley disagreed with this assertion.

Nestorius[95] never intended to launch a heretical movement; indeed, his dispute with Cyril of Alexandria[96] was not about theology; it was about conflicting personalities. Nevertheless, those who followed and modified the teachings of Nestorius soon developed a heretical movement that, in many quarters, can still be recognized in the Church today. Nestorius attempted to answer a very *simple* question: since Jesus is God, is it proper for us to say that the Virgin Mary is "The Mother of God?" (otherwise known as the θεοτοκος— *theotokos*—or "God bearer.") Most people who want to deny this title for Mary will say something like: "Mary was the mother of Jesus as a human being, but not of Jesus as God." This is Nestorianism. Full-blown Nestorians likewise argue that Jesus didn't suffer and die on the cross *as God,* but only as a human being. They argue that Jesus worked miracles as God, walked on the water as God, raised the dead as God ... did all his miraculous signs as God but not as a human being. As a human being, Jesus was tempted in the wilderness, grew hungry, wept, ate and drank, and prayed. All of his bodily actions were human, while all of his spiritual actions were divine.[97]

This division of labor between Jesus' human and divine natures is the theological essence of Nestorianism. It divides the human nature from the divine nature and, in so doing, it divides Jesus' salvific acts in his death and resurrection from us. Put simply, if Jesus suffered and died on the cross *only* as a human, with the divine nature not participating in his passion, then Jesus' death only had meaning and significance for *him.* It takes the consubstantial character of Jesus' humanity and divinity—both natures acting together in *all* things—for the benefits of his sacrifice to reach us. This means that it is impossible, when using orthodox theological terms, for us to say that Jesus did something as a human being but not as God. He did

---

[95]   The Patriarch ("Bishop") of Constantinople during the reign of Emperor Theodosius II (408–450 A.D.)

[96]   The Patriarch ("Bishop") of Alexandria, Egypt (412–444 A.D.), one of the most influential Church Fathers during the Christological controversies of the later 4th and early 5th centuries.

[97]   Brown, 173-174

everything as both God and as a human being.[98] Hence, when Jesus healed the sick, raised the dead, cast out demons, and fed the five thousand, both his divine nature and his human nature were present and active.

Likewise, when Jesus wept, was tempted in the wilderness, suffered and died on the cross, and was raised from the dead, both his human and divine natures were present and active. This is not "Patripassianism,"[99] for it is not God the Father in his fullness who died for us, but God the Son alone in his consubstantial humanity and divinity as Jesus of Nazareth, who died. God experienced death for us in Jesus Christ; the "Father," the first person of the Holy Trinity, did not die. Neither is this "Monophysitism,"[100] for it recognizes the reality of the two separate yet consubstantial natures of Jesus—full humanity and full divinity.

This is the kind of confusion that can result from Zwingli's approach to the question of the presence of Jesus in the Eucharist. A division and delineation of ability between what Jesus as God can do as opposed to what Jesus as a human can do will, inexorably, lead to a division of the salvific acts of the human Jesus on the cross from the salvific nature of God. While not intended, this is the result of the claim that Jesus is not present in the sacrament because his human nature cannot be everywhere.

Periodically, one sees Methodists asserting that the Zwinglian approach is identical to John Wesley's, because Wesley harshly criticized both the Roman Catholic and the Lutheran approach to the doctrine of Real Presence. This assertion is mistaken, however,

---

[98] This is the conclusion of the Fourth Ecumenical Council at Chalcedon (451 A.D.) and is still the position of the vast majority of Roman Catholics, Eastern Orthodox, and mainline Protestants today. As some slightly more jaded historians and theologians might say, this is the party that won. I prefer to view it as the party that struck a crucial balance in the light of prevailing political currents and, hence, survived. See: Brown, 180–181.

[99] The belief that God the Father died for our sins.

[100] The belief that Jesus' humanity and divinity are one in nature. There is a very fine line of distinction here between a united nature—human and divine—and a consubstantial nature. Some consider the distinction artificial, but I disagree. Maintaining consubstantiality ensures that we don't misunderstand Jesus' divinity as being somehow less divine than the Father's divinity, or Jesus' humanity as being somehow less human than our humanity.

because Wesley was also harshly critical of the Zwinglian approach. We will address Wesley's understanding of Real Presence in the next section.

The sacramental approach to the nature and function of Holy Communion, and particularly the idea of sacramental presence, will consume a significant portion of the remainder of this chapter. For now, suffice it to say that the Zwinglian/Memorial understanding of the Sacrament of Holy Communion has been the minority opinion throughout much of the last two thousand years. Most Christians have had a means of grace/Real Presence understanding of the Eucharist, and it is to this approach that we will now turn.

Real Presence

The cup of blessing that we bless, is it not a sharing in the blood of Christ?
The bread that we break, is it not a sharing in the body of Christ?
—1 Corinthians 10:16

Real Presence is the approach to the sacrament maintained by those denominations that affirm the concept of instrumental means. Holy Communion is a true, efficacious sacrament through which we are granted the strength, the transforming presence, and the life-changing grace of Jesus. Throughout the history of the Church, when the great theologians have expounded upon the nature of the sacrament, the concept of the real presence of Jesus has been the approach that has predominated. Indeed, it is exceedingly difficult to find any major—or even any minor—figure from the first fifteen hundred years of the Church who wrote about the Eucharist in terms other than that of Real Presence. While it is true that Thomas Aquinas didn't offer his complete formulation of the Roman Catholic Church's doctrine of transubstantiation until the sixteenth century, it is also undeniably true that the doctrine of our Lord's Real Presence in the Holy Meal had been around for at least fourteen centuries prior. It stands as, by far, the most ancient way of understanding the nature of the sacrament.

The writings of the Ante- and Post-Nicene Church Fathers are replete with references to the real presence of Jesus in the Lord's Supper. Take, for example, the stark literalism of John Chrysostom[101] who, while preaching a sermon on the meaning of the sixth chapter of the Gospel of John, said:

> [Christ] has made it possible for those who desire, not merely to look upon Him, but even to touch Him and to consume Him and to fix their teeth in His Flesh and to be commingled with Him... [102]

The imagery is both graphic and shocking, particularly in the bishop's startling reference to "fixing" one's "teeth" in Jesus' flesh. Chrysostom's words really are not any more shocking, however, than Jesus' own words upon which the bishop was reflecting:

> Those who eat my flesh and drink my blood have eternal life, and I will raise them up on the last day; for my flesh is true food and my blood is true drink.[103]

Another example of the patristic use of real presence language comes from Ignatius of Antioch[104], who in about 110 A.D. wrote:

> I have no taste for corruptible food nor for the pleasures of this life. I desire the bread of God, which is the flesh of Jesus Christ, who was of the seed of

---

[101]   John Chrysostom (347–407 A.D.), Archbishop of Constantinople. Chrysostom means "golden-mouthed," an epithet that was applied to him because of his brilliance as a preacher. His contribution to the development of Eucharistic liturgy cannot be over-emphasized.

[102]   Schaff, vol. 13, *Chrysostom, Homily 46*.

[103]   John 6:54–55

[104]   Ignatius of Antioch (50–117 A.D.), third Bishop of Antioch and a student of John the Apostle.

David; and for drink I desire his blood, which is love incorruptible.[105]

Even the highly metaphorical Ante-Nicene theologian Origen[106], while also reflecting upon John 6, makes this remarkably literal observation:

> Formerly, in an obscure way, there was manna for food; now, however, in full view, there is the true food, the flesh of the Word of God, as he himself says: "My flesh is true food, and my blood is true drink"[107]

The important point to be gathered from these several references is that graphic language affirming the real presence of Jesus is not limited to the later development of medieval Roman Catholicism. Quite the contrary, the idea that Jesus is made *really* present in, through, and by means of the sacramental elements of bread and wine is truly ancient, predating all later attempts at explaining the mechanism of *how* Jesus is made really present.

The Roman Catholic understanding of Real Presence is governed by the doctrine of transubstantiation, which teaches that the substance of the bread and wine are transformed into the literal, corporeal body and blood of Jesus. The bread becomes his flesh, and the wine becomes his blood, while both still retaining the look, smell, feel, and taste of bread and wine. The metaphysical "substance" of the bread and wine—wheat and grapes in their ontological nature—is transformed into the metaphysical "substance" of Christ's body and blood. In this way Roman Catholics believe that, when one receives Holy Communion, that person can be said to be receiving the real

---

[105]   Roberts, vol. 1, *Ignatius of Antioch, Letter to the Romans 7:3.*
[106]   Origen (184–254 A.D.) was from Alexandria but did his most important work while in Caesarea.
[107]   ibid. vol. 1, *Origin, Homilies on Numbers 7:2.*

presence of Jesus Christ and all the grace that his divine presence brings.[108]

Hildebert de Lavardin, Archbishop of Tours in the eleventh century, was the first to use the term *transubstantiation* in affirming sacramental real presence.[109] His use of the word, as well as many subsequent references to it over the following couple of centuries, lacked the foundations in Aristotelian philosophy that would later be developed in the middle of the thirteenth century by Thomas Aquinas. For example, the first conciliar use of the term comes from 1215 A.D. and the Confession of Faith of the Fourth Lateran Council:

> [Jesus'] body and blood are truly contained in the sacrament of the altar under the forms of bread and wine, the bread and wine having been transubstantiated, by God's power, into his body and blood.[110]

Here we find a simple statement of the idea that Jesus is somehow really present in the bread and the wine; no mechanism for the change is proposed, no philosophical arguments are applied, nor is anything asserted regarding the outward appearance (or "accidents") of the bread and wine remaining unchanged. The term is being used simply as a synonym for the change of the bread and the wine into the body and blood of Jesus.

With its formulation by Thomas Aquinas, and its eventual proclamation by the Council of Trent in 1551, transubstantiation became *the* Roman Catholic way of articulating and explaining the functional mechanism behind the doctrine of Real Presence in the Sacrament of Holy Communion. Over the centuries it has received a significant amount of criticism from Protestants, including

---

[108] James T. O'Conner, *The Hidden Manna: A Theology of the Eucharist* (Ignatius Press, 1988), 270–287.

[109] John Cuthbert Hedley, *Holy Eucharist* (Kessinger Publishing, 2010), 37.

[110] O'Conner, 185.

Methodists and Anglicans. Indeed, in the Articles of Religion we find a very harsh indictment of the concept:

> Transubstantiation, or the change of the substance of bread and wine in the Supper of our Lord, cannot be proved by Holy Writ, but is repugnant to the plain words of Scripture, overthroweth the nature of a sacrament, and hath given occasion to many superstitions.[111]

Interestingly enough, even some recent Roman Catholic theologians have recognized a degree of difficulty with the Aristotelian conception of "substance" in their doctrine. For example, Englebert Gutwenger, author of the Roman Catholic *Encyclopedia of Theology*, has reformulated transubstantiation thusly:

> The meaning of a thing can be changed without detriment to its matter. A house, for instance, consists of a certain arrangement of materials and has a clearly established nature and a clearly established purpose. If the house is demolished and the materials used for building a bridge, a change of nature or essence has intervened. Something completely different is there. The meaning has been changed, since a house is meant to be lived in and a bridge is used to cross a depression. But there has been no loss of material. [112]

Gutwenger goes on to assert that this can be seen as an analogy for the presence of Jesus in the bread and wine. Through consecration, the

---

[111] Article XVIII, The Methodist Articles of Religion, *The Book of Discipline of The United Methodist Church, 2012*; Article XXVIII, The Anglican Articles of Religion, *The Book of Common Prayer*.

[112] Englebert Gutwenger, *Encyclopedia of Theology*, (New York: Crossroad Publishing Co., 1976), 1754.

bread has been changed from something which was natural into "the dwelling-place and the symbol of Christ."[113] This new way of looking at real presence may make the Roman Catholic approach substantially closer to the several various Protestant catholic approaches, and it is certainly less objectionable—though how the Anglican theologians of the Reformation would have interpreted such a re-articulation of the Roman Catholic theory is a matter of speculation. Nevertheless, the fact remains that a real material change is still assumed by Roman Catholic Eucharistic theology, and this change continues to be articulated in the terms of Thomistic transubstantiation.

Roman Catholics, along with many Protestants (frequently from the Zwinglian perspective), have so closely identified transubstantiation with the very concept of real presence that they can no longer discern any difference. Indeed, it has been recognized in the many conversations between Rome and other denominations that Real Presence is a *common* affirmation of faith.[114] Its truth is *not* dependent upon any one formulation or way of speaking about it; historically, there have always been *several* accepted ways of talking about Real Presence.

While many Lutherans have changed their thinking concerning Real Presence, the traditional Lutheran approach is still consubstantiation. Essentially, the idea is that *along with* the bread and the wine is found the real body and blood of Jesus. Martin Luther spoke of the sacramental bread of Holy Communion as being *fleischbrot* ("fleshbread"), which he understood as being a new single substance formed out of the two substances of bread and our Lord's body.[115] For Luther, the real presence of Jesus is enabled by the ubiquity—as a shared virtue with divinity—that the human body of our Lord has in glory. Luther believed that the bodily presence of Jesus is made real and effectual within the elements of bread and

---

[113]   ibid.

[114]   *Baptism, Eucharist, and Ministry.* (Geneva: World Council of Churches, 1982), 12.

[115]   Gerrish, 165.

wine, and by this real presence the believer receives the grace and peace of Jesus' love.[116]

Clearly, Luther's formulation of consubstantiation affirms Real Presence in a way that *is no less* real and *no less* grace-filled than transubstantiation. It is simply the traditional, historic Lutheran way of speaking about how Jesus is really present in the sacrament. The idea of holy mystery is still present, for *how* the Holy Spirit causes the addition of the body and blood of Jesus to the elements of bread and wine is left open for various interpretations. It simply *happens*.

Something similar can be said regarding the Calvinist approach to Real Presence. It *is* true that the concept of sacramental instrumentality is sometimes doubted in Calvinism due, in large part, to the fundamental nature of the doctrines of limited atonement, irresistible grace, and the overall importance of predestination in their system. However, John Calvin's belief regarding the presence of Jesus in Holy Communion is beyond question. His own words are too eloquent to paraphrase:

> Now if anyone asks me how (*de modo*), I will be ashamed to admit that the mystery (*aracanum*) is too sublime for my intelligence to grasp or my words to declare: to speak more plainly, I experience rather than understand it. Here, then, without any arguing, I embrace the truth of God in which I may safely rest content. Christ proclaims that his flesh is the food, his blood the drink, of my soul. I offer him my soul to be fed with such food. In his sacred supper he bids me take, eat, and drink his body and blood under the symbols of bread and wine: I have no doubt that he truly proffers them and that I receive them.[117]

---

[116]   Brown, 318–319.

[117]   Gerrish, 174.

Essentially, the Calvinist approach is one of a *spiritual* real presence. This should not be misunderstood as suggesting a lack of actual presence, however, for Calvin linked the spiritual nature of Jesus' real presence with the deeper reality of divine sovereignty.[118] Jesus is present in the sacrament, in an efficacious way, through the holy mystery of God's almighty power. The disagreements among the various Calvinists regarding the instrumental nature of the sacrament as a means of grace has left Calvinism open for severe attack on several grounds; however, Calvin himself was clear: Jesus is really present, even if he couldn't articulate how. This is, essentially, the position of the Presbyterians, as well as of some, but certainly not all, Reformed Churches.

Ironically, the same is true for the Anglican/Methodist approach, which affirms that the presence of Jesus Christ is *real* but refuses to adopt any particular way, mechanism, or theory as to *how* his presence is real—it simply *is*. This similarity in affirmation has led some Wesleyan theologians to assert that the sacramental theology of the Wesley brothers was entirely Calvinist. I believe that this is an oversimplification of the Wesleyan approach. Yes, John and Charles Wesley both shared much of Calvin's awe for the mystery of Jesus' presence in the sacrament, but their affirmation of Real Presence stems far more from the complex integrative nature of Anglican sacramental thought than it did from the Calvinist elements within that thought. [119]

A good illustration of the Anglican/Methodist way of speaking about Real Presence can be seen in the wonderful Wesley Hymn, "O the depth of love divine." It begins with:

> O the depth of love divine,
> > the unfathomable grace!
> Who shall say how bread and wine

---

[118] ibid., 175

[119] Rob L. Staples, *Outward Sign and Inward Grace: The Place of the Sacraments in Wesleyan Spirituality* (Kansas City: Beacon Hill Press of Kansas City, 1991).

> God into us conveys!
> How the bread his flesh imparts,
>   how the wine transmits his blood,
> Fills his faithful people's hearts
>   with all the life of God![120]

Firstly, it should be noted that, for Charles Wesley, the *method* by which the elements convey the flesh and blood of Jesus Christ is a total mystery. Hence, Wesley wrote the words, "who shall say how bread and wine God into us conveys;" which, in contemporary English, would more correctly be phrased "who shall say how bread and wine conveys God into us!" No one can *really* say. Many Christians have their own ideas and opinions; many Churches have their own theories. The Roman Catholics have their own theory, and the Lutherans have one too; but like John Calvin, Anglicans and Methodists make no official proclamation as to *how* Jesus is present in the sacrament. In his hymn, Wesley is asserting that all the various explanations and theories are, essentially, *human* ways of trying to affirm what is fundamentally believed by all of those concerned (i.e., those who affirm Real Presence).

Secondly, it should be noted that the elements of bread and wine *convey*—one might even say "contain"—the flesh and blood of Jesus. I find it interesting that Wesley used the word "transmit" to describe the conveyance. If we think of that word as it is usually understood today—the ephemeral sending of information via electromagnetic waves—we can begin to see the depth of the meaning behind the statement that the elements "transmit" to us the flesh and blood of Jesus. Just as your telephone sends your voice from your end of the line to the other without becoming your voice, so also the elements transmit the presence of Jesus to the believer when the believer eats and drinks with faith.

The second stanza continues these thoughts:

---

[120]   UM *Hymnal*, 627.

Let the wisest mortals show
> how we the grace receive;
Feeble elements bestow
> a power not theirs to give.
Who explains the wondrous way,
> how through these the virtue came?
These the virtue did convey,
> yet still remain the same.[121]

Firstly, notice that the elements are said to have no virtue in and of themselves to convey the "power not theirs to give." It is a total and eternal mystery *how* God conveys the divine grace, either through prayer and the reading of Scripture or through the act of faith in eating and drinking bread and wine. It is *all* a mystery of God's self-giving love and of no merit to the vehicles which convey the grace.

Secondly, we should note that the elements of bread and wine do *truly* convey the real divine presence of Jesus Christ, and "yet remain the same." The bread remains bread and the wine remains wine. Their substance, according to the Anglican/Methodist approach to the sacraments, is not in any ontological way transformed; and yet, Christ is *still* truly present to and for us when we eat and drink with faith. The strength of this affirmation can be seen articulated even in the Articles of Religion, where it says regarding the question of how Jesus is present:

> The body of Christ is given, taken, and eaten in the Supper, only after a heavenly and spiritual manner. And the mean whereby the body of Christ is received and eaten in the Supper is faith.[122]

---

[121] ibid.

[122] Article XVIII, The Methodist Articles of Religion, *The Book of Discipline of The United Methodist Church, 2012*; Article XXVIII, The Anglican Articles of Religion, *The Book of Common Prayer.*

Granted, this article has been frequently misunderstood. Thanks to the ambiguity of its language, in which it states that the body of Christ is received in the sacrament "only after a heavenly and spiritual manner," some have taken it to mean that the presence of Christ is not "real" but merely "symbolic." This, however, is a *total* misreading of the article, failing largely due to a lack of understanding regarding the philosophical world-view of the framers of the Articles of Religion. Those who wrote the Articles believed that things which are "heavenly and spiritual" are *more* real than things which are "earthly and carnal." To say that Jesus is received in a "heavenly and spiritual manner" is to *actually* say that his presence is received in a way which is *more* real than the mere physical reception of the elements of bread and wine.

For Anglicans and Methodists the reality of the presence of Jesus as received through the sacramental elements is not in question. Real Presence is simply accepted as being true, its mysterious nature being affirmed and even lauded in official statements like *This Holy Mystery: A United Methodist Understanding of Holy Communion.*[123] Nevertheless, the question remains as to whether we should only say that the elements "convey" Real Presence, or if it is possible for us to affirm them as also *being* that presence. And, is there a difference between affirming the elements as mysteriously being the real presence and affirming bodily presence?

Of note among the Anglican theologians, John Wesley had significant difficulty in affirming the bodily presence of Jesus in the sacrament. While eager to affirm that the elements *are* the real presence of Jesus in an ontological fashion that goes beyond our

---

[123]   First approved by the General Conference of The United Methodist Church in 2004 as the denomination's first official, comprehensive statement on the meaning and practice of the Sacrament of Holy Communion. It was reaffirmed by the 2012 General Conference.

comprehension,[124] when his mother, Susannah, challenged him on this issue in a February 1732 letter,[125] John Wesley responded:

> ...we cannot allow Christ's human nature to be present in it, without allowing either con- or transubstantiation.[126]

Wesley's conclusion is warranted neither by Anglican theology nor even by his other affirmations regarding the nature of the Eucharist. Indeed, if we affirm Real Presence as a mysterious working of the Holy Spirit, nothing restricts us from affirming that the same may be equally true for bodily presence. The question of ubiquity, which was so very important when it came to Zwinglian theology and Luther's approach to Real Presence, is entirely beside the point. The human nature of Jesus has access to the ubiquity of our Lord's divine nature; and while Wesley never affirmed the sharing of attributes from Jesus' divine to Jesus' human nature, nevertheless such a conclusion is theologically sound and in keeping with Anglican thought in general. Sound Christology asserts that, while performing a miracle, the human nature of Jesus can be said to act *by virtue of* the divine nature; on the other hand, while living and experiencing things as a human being the divine nature can be said to act or share in the experience *by virtue of* the human nature. Both natures are unquestionably present, one by virtue of the other; and Wesley affirmed that it is the divine nature of Christ that makes Jesus really present in the Eucharist. Hence, while he squirmed at the idea of bodily presence, it is at best a fine line of distinction between Jesus being present through his divine nature and Jesus being bodily present. Therefore, the bodily presence of Jesus—a problem for Wesley, who was confronted

---

[124]   John Wesley, Letter to Mrs. Susanna Wesley (Feb. 28, 1731/2), Letters I, ed. Frank Baker, vol. 25 of *The Bicentennial Edition of the Works of John Wesley* (Nashville: Abingdon Press, 1976–), 328.

[125]   Wesley, Letter from Mrs. Susanna Wesley (Feb. 21, 1731/2), Works, 25: 326.

[126]   Wesley, Letter to Mrs. Susanna Wesley (Feb. 28, 1731/2), Works, 25: 328.

with the elaborate con- and transubstantial theories in the midst of reformation polemics—need not be a problem for us.

One way of thinking about this can be seen in how Christians affirm that the Scriptures contain the Word of God. The Holy Bible doesn't have Jesus within it … and, yet, it does! Holy Communion doesn't have Jesus within it … and, yet, it does! Jesus is the Word of God, incarnate in human flesh; the Bible is the Word of God, incarnate in human language; Holy Communion is the Word of God, incarnate in bread and wine.

This conception of the sacrament can be seen affirmed in the Eucharistic prayers that are common among both Methodists and Anglicans. In the *Book of Common Prayer* we find the following *epiclesis*[127] in Rite 2, Prayer A:

> Sanctify them [the gifts of bread and wine] by your Holy Spirit to be for your people the Body and Blood of your Son, the holy food and drink of new and unending life in him. Sanctify us also that we may faithfully receive this holy Sacrament, and serve you in unity, constancy, and peace….[128]

Prayer B contains an *epiclesis* that is fundamentally the same as this one. In Prayer C, however, the consecration reads even more clearly:

> Sanctify them by your Holy Spirit to be the Body and Blood of Jesus Christ our Lord.[129]

While it may not be a surprise to most Episcopalians that such a clear affirmation of Real Presence can be found in their Eucharistic prayers, it may come as a *real surprise* to some United Methodists

---

[127]   *Epiclesis*: Greek for "invocation." In Communion liturgies the epiclesis is that part of the prayer where the Holy Spirit is called upon to consecrate the elements.

[128]   *Book of Common Prayer*, Rite 2, Prayer A, 363.

[129]   *Book of Common Prayer*, Rite 2, Prayer C, 371.

that similar, equally unambiguous language can also be found in *The United Methodist Hymnal*. For example, the *epiclesis* found in the church's principle communion liturgy, *Word and Table I*, reads:

> Pour out your Holy Spirit on us gathered here, and on these gifts of bread and wine. Make them be for us the body and blood of Christ, that we may be for the world the body of Christ, redeemed by his blood.[130]

The language of these three Eucharistic prayers is unmistakable. In prayer to God, sacramental Protestants of the Anglican and Methodist families are asking the Holy Spirit to come upon the elements and "make them be for us the body and blood of Christ." This is not symbolism. This is *not* signification. This is not magic or superstition. This is *Real Presence* ... the real, divine, *bodily* presence of our Lord and Savior, Jesus Christ. It *could* be understood as transubstantiation, although such was neither implied nor intended by either the Anglicans or the Methodists. It could also be consubstantiation, although again such was not the intention of those who authored these liturgies. Here we find, with beauty unexplained, Jesus' efficacious presence being proclaimed. It is a presence that makes real for and within us the life-giving grace of God for, as is articulated in both the Episcopalian and Methodist prayers, the body of Christ in the sacrament makes us the Body of Christ for the world.

This affirmation of Real Presence can also be seen in the words of yet another wonderful Wesley Hymn: "Come Sinners to the Gospel Feast."

> Come and partake the gospel feast,
>   be saved from sin, in Jesus rest;
> O taste the goodness of our God,
>   and eat his flesh and drink his blood.[131]

---

[130]   *UM Hymnal*, 12.
[131]   *UM Hymnal*, 616.

This may well be the strongest, least ambiguous profession of Jesus' real presence to be found in Anglican and Methodist theology. It proclaims that Christ's presence in the elements of bread and wine is *real,* and that when we eat and drink the sacrament we are receiving the grace which is able to save us from our sins. The part of this stanza that shocks most Protestants, however, are the words from its final line: "…and eat his flesh and drink his blood." Protestants simply don't talk like that! Or, so I've been told.

I'll never forget the first time I assigned this hymn to be sung in a little country church. It was a wonderful congregation filled with many blessed, intelligent, hard working and deeply loving people. They had greeted me with open arms and had even accepted my little idiosyncrasies. I had been their pastor for only half a month, however, and so I had not yet realized that their sacramental understanding wasn't much deeper than "Let us break bread together on our knees." This is not at all an insult; it's just that, as I quickly discovered, we spoke a different language.

The first stanza of the hymn didn't bother them, and neither did the second. Oh sure, they had never sung this one before—as I had been told, at least two dozen times before the service that morning—but they were giving this "new" hymn a rousing first-time try, until the end of the third stanza.

I sang the fourth and fifth stanzas of the hymn on my own; even the pianist had quit playing, and as I looked up I noticed that all eyes were upon me, jaws had fallen to the floor, and eyebrows had been raised to the rafters. They simply couldn't believe, as I was later told, that such a hymn could even be in their hymnal, much less that I would have them sing it! Several of the congregation members were painfully polite to me the rest of that morning, and that evening I had a most interesting phone call from my District Superintendent.

"They said you were teaching Popish doctrine."

"Oh?" I replied, trying to suppress a chuckle.

"Yes. They said you had them sing a hymn that talked about eating the flesh and blood of Jesus. Did you?"

"Yes."

"Why did you do that?"

"Well … it's in the hymnal."

"Our hymnal? The 1989 *United Methodist Hymnal*? That's impossible."

"No, not at all. Look at number 616, the third stanza."

I sat in silence while the District Superintendent got out his hymnal and flipped through the pages until he came to the proper hymn. After a moment, I heard him mutter, "Well, I'll be…. You're right. I never noticed this one before."

Neither have many other United Methodist clergy. And, yet, these words have been in this Wesley hymn since Charles penned it in 1747; it has been in Methodist Hymnals since 1786. Granted, it is difficult to be more graphic or more literal than: "and eat his flesh and drink his blood." We are encouraged to "taste the goodness of our God,"[132] an image which brings home to us the tangible, experiential immediacy of divine presence in the sacrament. Likewise, we are told to "partake the Gospel feast," and, in so doing, "be saved from sin," and "in Jesus rest." This illustrates that the sacrament is far more than just a memorial meal, it is a means of justifying grace. When we partake of the Lord's Supper we are exercising our faith in the totality of what is sometimes called the "Christ Event"—our Lord's incarnation and birth through his life and his teachings to his suffering, crucifixion, death, burial, and resurrection. The "Gospel Feast" is all of this, and more. When we partake of the Blessed Sacrament as an act of faith, we are reaching out to touch the One who died for us. We are, by faith, receiving Christ into ourselves anew and are, in turn, received by Christ into the family of God. All of this is *part* of what we mean when we speak about the Eucharist being a means of grace; but it doesn't stop here. The fourth stanza reads:

> See him set forth before your eyes;
> behold the bleeding sacrifice;

---

[132] Taken from Psalm 34:8a – "O taste and see that the LORD is good.…"

his offered love make haste to embrace,
and freely now be saved by grace.[133]

Again, the imagery is powerful. "See him set forth before your
eyes"! On the altar before us can be found the "bleeding sacrifice"
of our Savior's divine presence. Yes, our eyes see bread and wine;
but our faith, having heard our Lord's words regarding the elements,
sees Jesus. And through receiving the sacrament we "embrace" the
"offered love" of Jesus and are "saved by grace." The sacrament is a
means of justifying grace – grace that saves, that delivers, that purges
us of sin and enables greater and greater expressions of faith within
us. But that's not all.

This embracing of our Lord's offered love is our response of faith
to the promises of Christ. Wesley, in yet another Eucharistic hymn,
speaks about the role of faith in our reception of the real presence of
Jesus in Holy Communion.

> FATHER, thy feeble Children meet,
> And make thy faithful Mercies known;
> Give us thro' Faith the Flesh to eat,
> And drink the Blood of CHRIST thy Son;
> Honour thine own mysterious Ways,
> Thy Sacramental Presence shew,
> And all the Fulness [*sic*] of thy Grace,
> With JESUS, on our Souls bestow.[134]

These words are no less surprising than those of the previous hymn,
while also being quite a bit more clear as to how Jesus is made known
to us in the sacrament. Indeed, it is ironic that, for a theologian who
had significant difficulty with the bodily presence of Jesus, Wesley
was still quite willing to utilize graphic bodily terms in speaking of

---

133   *UM Hymnal*, 616.
134   John and Charles Wesley, *Hymns on the Lord's Supper* (Madison, NJ: The Charles Wesley
       Society, 1995), 128.

Real Presence. "Give us thro' Faith the Flesh to eat, And drink the Blood of CHRIST thy Son" illustrates that the sacramental presence, manifested in the fullness of God's grace, comes to us when we eat and drink the elements with faith. Likewise, "Honour thine own mysterious Ways, Thy Sacramental Presence shew," affirms that, regardless of whatever theological speculations we may feel compelled to offer, in the end the sacramental presence of Jesus remains a mystery within our ability to experience but beyond our ability to comprehend. And, finally, "... all the Fulness [*sic*] of thy Grace, With JESUS, on our Souls bestow" brings home the realization that all of God's unmerited favor sweeps Jesus into our full being—into our souls, not just our stomachs.

This theme—that of faith as the portal through which we both discern and receive the real presence of Jesus—is continued in the second stanza of this hymn, where we offer ourselves to Christ:

> Father, our Sacrifice receive,
> Our Souls and Bodies we present,
> Our Goods, and Vows, and Praises give,
> Where'er they bounteous Love hath lent,
> Thou can'st not now our Gift despise,
> Call on that all atoning Lamb,
> Mixt with that bleeding Sacrifice,
> And offer'd up thro' JESU's Name.[135]

When we approach the holy table to receive the sacrament, by faith we are presenting our very selves to Jesus as a sacrifice for God's use. This idea is far beyond simple justification; it is the very embodiment of sanctification. We trust in God's grace and expect that *we* will be transformed into the Body of Christ. Indeed, this idea echoes the before-mentioned words of John Chrysostom, who affirmed that through receiving the Sacrament we become commingled with

---

[135]   ibid.

Christ. When we partake of the Eucharist, divine grace so infuses our being that we are changed, transformed, converted; we become, through repetitive reception, more and more like Christ as more and more of Christ's presence lives in and through us. Fundamentally, Holy Communion so unites us with the love of God that Christ's righteousness isn't just imputed to us, it is actually imparted within our living. By grace we are not only saved but are, indeed, transformed into the likeness of Jesus. And, as always, it occurs with, by, and for faith—the faith with which we see, know, and experience Jesus.

The idea of faith being involved in our discernment of the real presence of Jesus in the sacrament is nothing new, nor is it unique to Protestant thought. It is an ancient Catholic concept which is not all that different from what was articulated by Augustine who, preaching in 411 A.D., had this to say on Real Presence:

> What you see is the bread and the chalice; that is what your own eyes report to you. But what your faith obliges you to accept is that the bread is the Body of Christ and the chalice is the Blood of Christ. This has been said very briefly, which may perhaps be sufficient for faith.[136]

The Wesley brothers are part of this very ancient stream of thought on the nature of the presence of Christ in the sacrament. By faith we discern the body and blood of Jesus in the bread and the cup. By faith we receive the body and blood of Jesus through the bread and the cup. And by faith we live as the body of Christ for a broken and hurting world. In the Eucharist we have God's grace functioning in a prevenient, justifying, and sanctifying manner; where we are in our Christian living will determine how the Eucharist forms, molds, transforms, and perfects us. But, so long as we partake of the sacrament with faith, there is no question that the real presence will

---

[136]   Schaff, vol. 4, *Augustine Sermon*, 227.

have an abiding, life changing impact upon us. While reason fails us in explaining how this is the case—it remains a holy mystery—nevertheless, this has been the tradition and experience of the Church since its very inception, something which the witness of the Scriptures also show.

Scriptural Foundations

> "Those who eat my flesh and drink my blood have eternal life,
> and I will raise them up on the last day...."
> —*John 6:54*

What are the Scriptural justifications, if any, for the concept of the real presence of Jesus in the Sacrament of Holy Communion? This is a valid question, and one that deserves serious consideration. Frequently, one is apt to hear Zwinglians say that the Scriptures do not support an understanding of the sacrament as being anything more than a memorial meal; they cite the Words of Institution—and particularly the phrase "Do this in remembrance of me."[137]—as if such were sufficient to demonstrate that the sacrament is nothing but a memorial. While it is true that memorial aspects are very much present in the Blessed Sacrament, it is nevertheless also true that far more is going on in the meal than just a memorial. This can be seen both in the Church's dogged persistence in affirming the doctrine, as well as in the many ringing affirmations of personal experience, like Calvin's, which have prompted Christians to proclaim the doctrine of Real Presence even if our minds could not comprehend the "how" of it as anything more than a holy mystery. But what, if anything, can we discern through Scripture concerning the nature of Holy Communion?

---

[137]   Luke 22:19b

In the Acts of the Apostles, for instance, we find a couple of references to "the breaking of bread" as being a central part of the worship life of the early Christian community.[138] Unfortunately, in Acts we are told next to nothing about how the New Testament Christians comprehended the nature and significance of these Communions. However, it is clear from Acts 20:7 that a worship service, with the celebration of the Lord's Supper, was observed on Sunday:

> On the first day of the week, when we met to break bread, Paul was holding a discussion with them; since he intended to leave the next day, he continued speaking until midnight.[139]

It appears from the context of this passage that meeting on the Lord's Day to celebrate the Eucharist was the usual practice for them and that Paul was simply taking the opportunity of the Lord's Day celebration to meet with the church and do some essential teaching. It is quite unlikely that this experience of Communion, which occurred at Troas in Asia Minor, differed either in meaning or in practice from the sacrament that Paul describes in his letter to the Corinthians. We can, therefore, confidently assume that in Corinth the Christians celebrated the Lord's Supper on Sundays; and that this was intended to be a time for scriptural interpretation and theological discussion as well as worship and praise.

Paul's only surviving teachings about the meaning and nature of Holy Communion can be found in 1 Corinthians 10:14-22 and 11:17-36. In the first passage we find the Apostle warning the Corinthians about the dangers of accommodating themselves to the infamous idolatry of their city.

---

[138]   Acts 2:42–46; 20:7
[139]   Acts 20:7

Therefore, my dear friends, flee from the worship of idols. I speak as to sensible people; judge for yourselves what I say. The cup of blessing that we bless, is it not a sharing in the blood of Christ? The bread that we break, is it not a sharing in the body of Christ? Because there is one bread, we who are many are one body, for we all partake of the one bread. Consider the people of Israel; are not those who eat the sacrifices partners in the altar? What do I imply then? That food sacrificed to idols is anything, or that an idol is anything? No, I imply that what pagans sacrifice, they sacrifice to demons and not to God. I do not want you to be partners with demons. You cannot drink the cup of the Lord and the cup of demons. You cannot partake of the table of the Lord and the table of demons. Or are we provoking the Lord to jealousy? Are we stronger than he?[140]

The Apostle is addressing the specific situation of the Corinthian Christians, who lived in a city where both Judaism and Christianity were extreme minorities among a multitude of pagan religious institutions. In that setting it was expected that a Gentile, in the course of engaging in economic, social, or political discourse, would partake of pagan religious feasts and practices. For example, completing a business contract might involve making a sacrifice at a pagan temple to "cement the deal."

Likewise, attending a social function might involve feasting on a sacrificed bull procured from a pagan temple. Or, being involved in city administration might well involve partaking in the ritual practices of the pagan temple which oversaw a particular activity. To put it simply, good Gentiles in Corinth were expected to involve themselves in the religious life of the city. Paul is saying that such

---

[140]   1 Corinthians 10:14–22

an intermixing should not take place, and he is doing so based upon an argument from analogy. Essentially, he opposes involvement in pagan religious feasts because those cultic meals were understood as a partaking in the life of the beings in whose honor they were held. Christians should not participate in such religious functions because, in the Eucharist, they already partake of the life of Jesus Christ.[141]

This is a *crucial* point; the analogy that Paul makes assumes that a *real* conveying of the life of Jesus occurs in the Eucharist—without such an understanding of the real presence of Jesus, the analogy collapses. Paul believed that Christian worship, in which the Lord's Supper is eaten, is a means of communicating and receiving the real presence of Jesus.[142]

Furthermore, to partake of the real presence of Christ is to partake of the very life of the community of faith—the "Body." As Paul wrote, "Because there is one bread, we who are many are one body."[143] The common loaf of bread is understood to stand for the ontological unity of all Christians. And, we are made one through the partaking of the bread of heaven, the sacrament of the Body of Christ. If we are one with each other in Christ Jesus, we cannot also be one with other religious communities. We must partake *only* of the Body of Christ, not the body of demons.

The next passage finds the Apostle addressing several serious irregularities in the Eucharistic practices among the Corinthian Christians:

---

[141]   Archibald Robertson and Alfred Plummer, *A Critical and Exegetical Commentary On The First Epistle of St. Paul to the Corinthians* (Edinburgh: T&T Clark, Limited, 1986 [reprint]), 212-213. Hans Conzelmann, *1 Corinthians* (Philadelphia: Fortress Press, 1975), 171–173.

[142]   For more on this conclusion, see a rare book by a former Archbishop of Canterbury, Michael Ramsey, *The Gospel and the Catholic Church* (Cambridge: Cowley Press, 1990 [Reprint]), 98–119. The Archbishop concludes, as do I, that this is a strong indicator of the Real Presence even within the writings of the Apostle Paul. Some scholars doubt this interpretation, but in my opinion if such a conclusion is not maintained there would be insufficient ground for maintaining the analogy. I wish I could claim this opinion as originally my own, but it is not; nor is it even original with the Archbishop. It is a long-standing Anglican interpretation, and one with which Wesley was familiar (see Wesley's *Notes on the NT* dealing with this verse, and observe his stress on the unitive nature of the sacrament).

[143]   1 Corinthians 10:14-22

For I received from the Lord what I also handed on to you, that the Lord Jesus on the night when he was betrayed took a loaf of bread, and when he had given thanks, he broke it and said, "This is my body that is for you. Do this in remembrance of me." In the same way he took the cup also, after supper, saying, "This cup is the new covenant in my blood. Do this, as often as you drink it, in remembrance of me." For as often as you eat this bread and drink the cup, you proclaim the Lord's death until he comes. Whoever, therefore, eats the bread or drinks the cup of the Lord in an unworthy manner will be answerable for the body and blood of the Lord. Examine yourselves, and only then eat of the bread and drink of the cup. For all who eat and drink without discerning the body, eat and drink judgment against themselves. For this reason many of you are weak and ill, and some have died.[144]

In this passage we find Paul affirming, with words that are hard to deny and must have been equally hard for the Corinthians to hear, that the real presence of Jesus in the sacrament and in the community of faith must be discerned. Indeed, failure to discern the presence of the Body of Christ is the very essence of what it means to partake in an unworthy manner, thus opening oneself to judgment.

This is why a personal examination prior to Communion is such a common practice in nearly all Christian communities. This is not a time to beat on oneself; it is a time of careful inner discernment, with our eyes focused intently upon Christ as our source of salvation and sanctification. When I engage in such a personal examination, I look within myself and at my own need of God's grace. It's an opportunity to make my own confession of sin to Christ, as well as being an important opportunity to work on breaking down any barriers, any

---

[144]   1 Corinthians 11:23-30

estrangements, which I may have built up between myself and others in the community. To properly discern the presence of Jesus in the Eucharist, I must first discern the presence of Jesus in my neighbor and in myself.

While this has already been said, it merits repeating. Paul's words in 1 Corinthians 11:23-33 have *nothing* to do with being worthy to partake of Holy Communion. Unfortunately, the way the passage reads in the King James Version has led some to think that this is speaking about one's own worthiness:

> For he that eateth and drinketh *unworthily*, eateth and drinketh damnation to himself, not discerning the Lord's body.[145]

This does not mean that we have to be worthy, or sinless, or even have all our sins confessed in order to partake of the sacrament. "Worthy" in this passage is used as an adverb, not an adjective, and modifies the action, not the actor. The manner of partaking is in question, *not* the one who is partaking. What we are called to examine is our focus as we partake. Are we focused on the love of Christ, upon his wonderful grace and the forgiveness that we have received from him for our sins; or are we focused, with gnashing teeth, upon the person several pews up whom we can't stand and wish weren't in our church? Are we focused on Jesus, or are we thinking "I've gotten rid of all those sins, and now I'm worthy to come to the table ... unlike those sinful jerks over there!"

These are the kinds of examinations that I believe Paul is really talking about. Are we recognizing the real presence of Jesus in our midst? Are we recognizing the Body of Christ within our fellow believers—even those we don't like? Or, are we denying the Body of Christ? Are we denying the real presence of Jesus? Are we denying the saving and transforming grace of our Lord? While these examinations

---

[145]   1 Corinthians 11:29, *KJV*, emphasis added.

do have an important personal dimension, the worthiness of the individual believer was *never* the question. The simple fact is that *no one* is worthy to receive the consecrated elements of our Lord's Body and Blood in the Sacrament of Holy Communion. Indeed, we come to the table precisely *because* we are unworthy and are in need of being made worthy by the blood of the Lamb. All we have to do is focus our faith upon the love, mercy, grace, peace, and real presence of Jesus and we will be receiving worthily. A confession of sin, and the self-examination that comes before such a confession, is an excellent way of doing this because it takes us out of the equation and focuses our attention upon the source of our forgiveness—Christ Jesus our Lord.

Through Holy Communion we proclaim our Lord's death; we also proclaim our own death to self. When we partake of the elements we receive into ourselves the means of grace which, working through our faith, unites us to the Body of Christ. We recognize our own radical need of grace, our lack of self-sufficiency, and the presence of Jesus within ourselves and within the community. Communion is our participation in the very Body of Christ, which is manifested for the entire world in God's people and for God's people in the broken bread and shared cup. Essentially, the Eucharist and the Body of Christ—the Church—are *inseparable*.

Moving on from the Apostle Paul, let's take a moment to look at the Gospel of John. Alone among the Gospels, it does not record the Words of Institution. While the Last Supper does take place within the narrative account, in place of the sacrament we find Jesus washing his disciples' feet—a ritual which has every characteristic of a sacrament or, in the very least, a means of grace. Rather than containing an account of the institution of the Lord's Supper, the entire Gospel is an exposition upon the meaning of the Blessed Sacrament. This is nowhere more true than in the lengthy and often controversial sixth chapter:

> I am the bread of life. Your ancestors ate the manna
> in the wilderness, and they died. This is the bread

that comes down from heaven, so that one may eat of
it and not die. I am the living bread that came down
from heaven. Whoever eats of this bread will live
forever; and the bread that I will give for the life of
the world is my flesh."

The Jews then disputed among themselves, saying,
"How can this man give us his flesh to eat?" So Jesus
said to them, "Very truly, I tell you, unless you eat the
flesh of the Son of Man and drink his blood, you have
no life in you. Those who eat my flesh and drink my
blood have eternal life, and I will raise them up on the
last day; for my flesh is true food and my blood is true
drink. Those who eat my flesh and drink my blood
abide in me, and I in them. Just as the living Father
sent me, and I live because of the Father, so whoever
eats me will live because of me. This is the bread that
came down from heaven, not like that which your
ancestors ate, and they died. But the one who eats this
bread will live forever."[146]

This has been a troubling passage for many Protestants; it is difficult
for us and for those who first heard it. "How can this man give us his
flesh to eat?" That is precisely what those who reject Eucharistic Real
Presence ask. How could Jesus give his disciples his flesh to eat and
his blood to drink? How could his flesh be "true food" and his blood
"true drink" when his flesh was still on his bones or his blood was
still flowing through his veins? More to the point for today, how can
Jesus give us his flesh as divine nourishment when his body is with
him, now, in glory?

Through the last few centuries some Protestant scholars have
suggested that this teaching refers not to the Sacrament of Holy
Communion as a means of grace but to the whole work of Christ,

---

[146]   John 6:48-58

from his incarnation and birth all the way through his life to his self-giving sacrifice and death upon the cross. The entire Christ event, as the supreme redemptive expression of God's love for all creation, is indicated when Jesus says "I am the bread of life."[147] And it must be admitted that their reasoning is rooted in an important truth: it is, indeed, our Lord's grace which feeds our hungry souls. We are starving for the divine bread of eternal life, a hunger that can only be satisfied by the real presence of Jesus. Many non-sacramental Protestants will argue that Jesus' words are best taken spiritually; sacramentalists prefer to read them as being *both* spiritual and literal. Real Presence is both a divine and a physical reality: it is communicated by the means of grace, embodied in the sacrament, and lived outwardly for the world by the Church. Regardless how one reads the passage it cannot be denied that the Evangelist highlights the fundamental place of the Eucharist in the life of the Church.

The intentional use of Eucharistic language in John 6 demonstrates how completely the fourth Gospel depends upon sacramental thought to articulate its interpretation of the life and ministry of Jesus. In one respect, this is appropriate; because, as several Eastern Orthodox theologians have reminded us, Jesus Christ *is* our Sacrament.[148] Nevertheless, it surely doesn't hurt to take note of the Eucharistic language in John 6. "Bread" and "eating," "blood" and "drinking" … these are all unmistakably explicit sacramental terms, each containing in their usage the anticipation of Eucharistic practice. For the author of John's Gospel to lean so heavily upon such blatantly Eucharistic language truly highlights the importance of the sacrament for the life of his community.[149]

In the above quoted section we find Jesus saying that "… the bread that I will give for the life of the world is my flesh."[150] This

---

[147]   John 6:48
[148]   Alexander Schmemann, *For The Life Of The World: Sacraments and Orthodoxy* (Crestwood: St. Vladimir's Press, 1988).
[149]   Ramsey, 105 – 107.
[150]   John 6:51

is fairly literal, and quite difficult. When those who were listening confronted him concerning his meaning, he was offered a wonderful opportunity to explain himself with "No, I mean that I am *like* the bread of heaven." But, no, Jesus doesn't soften his words at all. Quite the contrary, he makes them more difficult. "Those who eat my flesh and drink my blood have eternal life."[151] Now, granted, when his disciples complained about the saying, Jesus asserted that "It is the spirit that gives life; the flesh is useless. The words that I have spoken to you are spirit and life."[152] John Wesley, like many before and since, latched on to this statement and in the light of it asserted:

> This whole discourse concerning his flesh and blood
> refers directly to his passion, and but remotely, if at
> all, to the Lord's Supper.[153]

Our Lord's death and the promise of our eternal life is, certainly, reflected throughout the verses of John 6. And yet, even recognizing this and focusing on this interpretation, Wesley nevertheless accepted that there might well be a place for understanding the Lord's Supper through the imagery contained in John 6. I believe that both approaches are correct. We can only understand the sacrament through the context—the interpretive lenses—of our Lord's life, death, and resurrection. And, likewise, we can only experience the real presence of Jesus when we open ourselves to our Lord's death with the willingness to die to ourselves so that we may live in Christ.

Additional imagery in John 6 points to Jesus' nature as our eternal sacrament. Here are only a few examples: in John 6:4, we find that the Passover was near; in John 6:11, Jesus gives thanks before distributing the loaves; in John 6:12-13 the feeding of the multitude is symbolic of the heavenly banquet of plenty, in which we will join

---

[151]   John 6:54
[152]   John 6:61
[153]   Wesley's *Notes on the NT*, John 6:51

in glory.[154] Jesus is the heavenly food of the banquet, the "marriage supper of the lamb."[155] He is the bread of heaven, and he nourishes his body, the Church, with his real presence.

Who or What is Transformed?

All of this leads us to two questions, and those who come from the sacramental perspective might find them helpful. Firstly, "who is transformed in the sacrament?" And, secondly, "what does Jesus' real presence mean for us?" I believe that both approaches to the nature of Holy Communion—Real Presence *and* Memorial Representation—have elements of truth to them. From the side of Real Presence, I believe that the important point is that the Eucharist is a *real,* efficacious means of grace through which Jesus is made truly present in a transforming, substance-changing way. When believers come to the table with faith and receive the bread and wine, they are receiving into themselves the grace of God which transubstantiates *them.*

In other words, I affirm that there *is* an ontological transformation of substance that occurs in Holy Communion. I do *not* believe that it is in a *literal* transformation of the bread and wine but, rather, that *through* the bread and wine comes a transformation of the congregation of believers. *We* are transformed—transubstantiated, if you will—into the Body of Christ. We may still look, smell, and probably even taste like mortal human beings, but we are really no longer individual Christians; we are part of the Body of Christ. And this points out where those who affirm Memorial Representation are also correct: the radical transformation that God's grace works is, in the end, within the believer and within and *through* the community of Faith.

Throughout the history of the church, and for Protestant catholics as well as Roman Catholics, Holy Communion has been the means

---

[154] John 6:26-27
[155] Revelation 19:9

of grace through which we are *re*-membered to—brought back into membership with—the Body of Christ. The reality of Jesus' divine, grace-giving presence in the Sacrament of Holy Communion must *not* be minimized. It is his presence which gives that eternal meal its power not only to justify but also to sanctify and perfect us.

* * *

I can remember sitting in the simple, uncomplicated, comfortable little chapel at St. John's House in Durham, North Carolina, on Saturday mornings, quietly reflecting upon the week which had passed me by as I smelled the incense burning, sang the Gloria, and listened as the scriptures were read. Those were moments of knowing the real presence of Jesus. Brother Paul would give a sermon which reached down into the very depths of my soul, and God would speak to me words of comfort and peace, words which would sustain me in the long hours of study and reflection in the week that was to come. Following the prayers, we would join the monks around the Altar for the Great Thanksgiving and Holy Communion, sure in our confidence that, with eyes and hearts of faith, our Savior was there to meet us. To this day, the memories of these experiences frequently flood my soul as I stand behind the table in my own chapel or sanctuary and pray the liturgy with upturned hands. In these holy moments I praise God for those wonderful men of faith, and for their ministry, which has had an enormous impact on my own.

I remember Brother Brian. He looked every bit the part of a "Friar Tuck;" we often called him "Father Elmer Fudd" for his perpetual grin, infectious sense of humor, and the simple fact that his singing voice sometimes reminded us of that cartoon character. And yet, Brian was anything but a whimsical cartoon character. He had a sharp wit that wouldn't quit, and an even sharper mind that could explicate Scripture and define Christian doctrine with the greatest of ease. He took everything he did in ministry with utter devotion and deep seriousness; and he would happily take time out to explain *why* thus-and-such was done *this* way and not some *other* way.

I'm not sure if Brian ever realized it, but the reality of my call to ministry was renewed many times by just watching him preach, iron sheets, celebrate Holy Communion, clean dishes in the kitchen, play with the monastery cats, and lead retreats. "Ministry is not something separated from life," Brian liked to say. "For the Christian, ministry is *inseparable* from life. Indeed, Greg, ministry *is* your life. Live it well."

One Saturday morning, following the Eucharist, a friend of mine and I remained in the chapel to help this brilliant, sometimes mischievous, monk clean up and prepare for noonday prayer. As we joined him consuming the left-over elements, my friend got up his courage to ask, "Father Brian, what do you whisper to the bread before Communion when you place it on the table? 'Don't worry, this won't hurt a bit.'"[156]

Brian, with his most serious face on, shook his head and said, "Oh, no! No! It did hurt! When Jesus hung on the cross and took our sins upon himself, it hurt him *very* much." Then, with a twinkle in his eye and a silly grin on his face, he added, "But the bread doesn't have any nerve endings."

We never did find out from him what those whispered words were. Oh, I've subsequently learned many of the quiet prayers that may be offered at the altar while preparing the bread and cup, and I find myself praying them as I set the table for celebration. However, even as I pray them—and as I raise my own hands and pray the Great Thanksgiving—I can't shake from my mind the twinkle in Brother Brian's eye that day or his joy at presiding in the Holy Mystery of the Table of the Lord. It's a joy which I now know and an awesome privilege which I am honored to share.

---

[156] That friend was the Reverend Paul B. Longmire. Paul is nearly as mischievous as Brother Brian.

Questions for Reflection and Discussion

Chapter Five

♦ If you can, describe the first time you received Holy Communion. Did it seem strange to you?

♦ What does Communion mean to you?

♦ How frequently do you receive Communion?

♦ Would you like to receive it more frequently?

♦ What is the meaning of Memorial Representation?

♦ What is the meaning of Real Presence?

♦ If you believe that Jesus is present in Communion, what does his presence there mean for you?

♦ Do you ever feel different when you receive Communion? If so, can you describe the difference?

♦ Have you ever been afraid to receive Communion? If so, why?

Transfigured Fear

Transform this fear I feel, O God.
Deliver me from my distress.
Relieve my soul of dread and loss.
Lift the cloud of hopeless dross.
And place your strong, strong back in mine,
To lift this heavy cross.

O Jesus, all you suffered not in vain.
I know you know my deepest pain.
I know you see my inner heart.
I know you feel hurts when they start.
In body, soul, and spirit now,
Transform my fear somehow.

"My God, my God, why?"
My fearful heart does cry,
In pain, when body joints do ache.
"I'm falling apart!" my voice does quake.
In mind and body, so distraught,
Against dreadful odds I've fought.

In dazzling brightness you did transform,
The humanly form of Jesus Lord,
From dust and clay to glorious God,
Present high on the mountain sod.
Please transfigure now my deepest fears,
And wipe away these bitter tears.

Gregory S. Neal †
Methodist Hospital, Dallas
January 18, 1997

Chapter Six

The Sacramentals as Means of Grace

T hroughout the long history of the Church, most Christians have recognized at least two dominical sacraments: Baptism and Holy Communion. Some denominations, particularly the Roman Catholic Church and those of the Eastern Orthodoxy, maintain that there are actually five additional sacraments, all of which function in a complimentary manner to the two principle sacraments. They are usually identified as: Confirmation, Penance, Marriage, Ordination, and Extreme Unction. While most Protestants have not recognized these five as being formal sacraments, several *are* often understood as being means of grace with some degree of sacramental character.

For example, according to ritual and practice, United Methodists incorporate the act of Confirmation into the liturgy of Baptism as constituting the Christian's response of faith to God's prevenient grace. Most other sacramental Churches also observe Confirmation, or a version of it. Something similar holds for Marriage and Ordination, as well as for various forms of the penitential rite and anointing with oil. Nevertheless, for the most part Protestants have been quite hesitant about using sacramental terminology for these other means of grace. While understood as instruments through which Christians receive God's love and presence, they are not usually understood as having the same sacramentality as Baptism and Holy Communion.

Among Protestants these additional means of grace are sometimes called "sacramentals" rather than "sacraments." The distinction is a very fine one, but it is worthy of note. Essentially, the sacramentals are those means of grace which have most, but not all, of the basic characteristics of a sacrament. In some cases the sacramentals simply lack having been *clearly* established by Jesus in Scripture. In most cases, however, the difference between the sacramentals and the sacraments is far more difficult to discern.

Like the sacraments, the sacramentals require a human response of faith for them to operate as effective means of grace. In this way, they stand out from the general means of grace and are worthy of special note. In this chapter, we will look at several of the most commonly recognized sacramentals, as well as a couple of means of grace which haven't been commonly thought of as having sacramental characteristics. While there are *many* more means than the ones we will examine in this book, all of those with which we will be dealing have significant sacramental qualities.

It should be noted that, while the Roman Catholic Church uses the term "sacramentals," they do not connect this term with any of the five means of grace that they identify as sacraments alongside Baptism and the Eucharist. Roman Catholics classify as being sacramentals those practices or traditions that provide help or comfort to Christians, especially within the context of worship. For example, making the sign of the cross is one of the sacramentals. The same is true for the various prayers that are offered by Christians at various points in the worship service, or the use of incense, or of holy water. These are all sacramentals, but they are not sacraments.

The sacramentals might be accurately referred to as "lesser," not "principle," sacraments. In some circles the term *Dominical* is applied to Baptism and Communion, highlighting the Lord's role in appointing them for our observance. The *Catechism* of the Roman Catholic Church even states that:

> Sacramentals are instituted for the sanctification of
> certain ministries of the Church, certain states of life,

a great variety of circumstances in Christian life, and
the use of many things helpful to man.[157]

While I believe that this definition is an excellent one, I also believe
that it applies to the five additional means of grace that Rome
identifies as sacraments. In addition to the means in this group, I also
believe that it applies to Giving and to the practice of Footwashing.

Since we have already addressed Confirmation within the
context of Baptism, we will proceed in this chapter to examine the
sacramentals of Forgiveness, Healing, Marriage, Ordination, Prayer,
Giving, and Footwashing. In each case, it is my conviction that what
we find here are means of grace that have many of the characteristics
of the primary sacraments but which lack at least some aspects of a
full sacramental character.

Forgiveness

> If you forgive the sins of any, they are forgiven them;
> if you retain the sins of any, they are retained.
> —*John 20:23*

While I was in Seminary I spent a year as a student chaplain
in Duke University Medical School's Clinical Pastoral Education
program. After my return to Texas, and while serving as Pastor of
an inner-city congregation in Dallas, I volunteered as an adjunct
chaplain at Methodist Hospital. Spending three nights a month "on
call" in a busy, big-city hospital like Dallas' Methodist Central gave
me new insights into the need for forgiveness.

Early one morning, at 3:30 am, the pager alerted me to an
approaching ambulance. I had been in bed for only a few minutes
and so it wasn't very difficult for me to get up. I put on my clothing,

---

[157]   The Roman *Catechism*, 415.

grabbed my pad, pager, Bible and stole, and headed out the door. I hurried because those being brought in might need spiritual help. They might need someone to pray with them, call family or friends, and help them communicate with the hospital staff. The spiritual and practical needs of those who are suffering through the trauma of an Emergency room visit are frequently great, and that's why I was there.

As I rode the elevator down the seven floors to the Emergency Room I wondered about what I was going to find there. The possibilities were almost endless, and what I usually found was hardly ever what I expected. It was a new adventure each and every time. From automobile accident to gunshot victim, each patient was different, with different needs, different fears, different hopes and different dreams. I have been welcomed by frightened people who had just been through a horrible experience and desired the comforting presence of God. I have been looked at with hatred by those who view all Christians as liars. Some on the hospital staff have considered me a nuisance, while others have considered me a "God-send." Indeed, I have had a weary-eyed nurse or physician turn to me when the evening has gone horribly bad in hopes of hearing a word of comfort or a word that might bring them some sense of sanity. The way a hospital chaplain is received can be as varied as there are days in the year and people in the world.

The need to be there was great, and so I went. I could easily recount the many times when all a patient needed was a gentle touch and helping hand. However, I could also easily tell of all those times when the patient was so close to death that the need for spiritual comfort and prayer was paramount.

As I walked into the department that morning, I put on the narrow purple stole that I carry for such occasions. I have found that wearing such a stole, in addition to a clerical collar, is one of the quickest ways to make it clear to the patients exactly who and what I am. If nothing else, these outward symbols of the Christian faith ease introductions and engender confidence. Thus prepared for the unknown, I began to make my way through the trauma center, stopping at various beds to speak for a moment with an injured soul or a frightened parent and child. Slowly, I made my way across the department, finally ending up in one of the emergency wards, where I found a team of doctors and nurses frantically working on a middle-aged woman.

As I walked into the room her head turned, her eyes caught mine, and her hand reached out for me. I stepped closer and she took my hand, pulled me down so that my ear was next to her lips, and in desperate, breathless words she gasped out a list of sins that had been plaguing her. Some of her sins were serious, some were not, but all of them were important enough to her that she expended her last few breaths in asking for forgiveness.

In that moment of her utter desperation, when her life was beginning to ebb away, I looked down into her pleading eyes and realized that I was peering into a soul in search of peace. She wasn't looking for healing, or for vain hope of continued life; she was after the blessed assurance that only God's forgiveness could bring. And so, in those final moments of her life, I offered her that assurance with the glorious words that Jesus gave us for this very purpose. I reached out my free hand and made the sign of the cross over her face where she could see it as I pronounced: "In the name of Jesus Christ, your sins are forgiven. Go in peace."

I'll never forget the look which crossed her face in that moment. No longer were her eyes pleading, full of desperation and fear. No, they were filled with a sense of thanksgiving and with the peace that comes from knowing that there is nothing to fear from God. Peace—the peace that comes from forgiveness—is our Lord's gift to us from the cross. And it was a gift that this woman received in the last moments of her life. This look of peace settled upon her face, and a smile appeared on her lips, as she died.

Standing there, looking down at this woman, I realized that I had just watched as our Lord had gathered her into his loving embrace. It was an awe-inspiring experience, and one that I will never forget. The words of forgiveness were what this woman needed to hear before she

could accept the peace that Jesus was offering her. My proclamation
of forgiveness served as a means of grace, as an instrument of God's
love, which enabled her to accept the gift that Jesus was offering her.
Forgiveness was already hers for the taking; this dying woman, like
so many others, simply needed to hear the Good News again. At the
moment of her death she needed to hear, one last time, that in the
name of Jesus Christ her sins were forgiven.

Forgiveness is a glorious gift from God, and sharing Christ's
forgiveness is a calling that *all* Christians have received. Apart
from Christ's grace, forgiveness is impossible; only God can truly
forgive sin. The wonderful good news is that through the love of God,
empowered within us by the Holy Spirit, all Christians are given the
authority to forgive others the sins that they have committed against
us, and indeed, against God. In dealing with the sins of others, the
Scriptures are clear:

> For if you forgive others their trespasses, your
> heavenly Father will also forgive you; but if you do
> not forgive others, neither will your Father forgive
> your trespasses.[158]

That this passage comes to us through the words of the "Lord's
Prayer" doesn't soften its impact on our lives—quite the contrary!
Being a forgiven people means that we are called to forgive others
their "trespasses" against us. Many of us pray the "Lord's Prayer"
every Sunday, but do we practice what we pray? Do we open ourselves
to God's grace through forgiveness? When we say that forgiveness
is a sacramental means of grace, do we understand that we are to
receive God's grace of forgiveness and then become conduits of
God's forgiving grace to others? Do we understand that when we
harbor grudges and refuse to forgive we also block God's grace in our

---

[158]   Matthew 6:14-15

lives? Do we realize that when we deny the grace of forgiveness we harm ourselves and close ourselves off to a measure of God's love?

Based upon my personal experience, I fear that we frequently behave as if none of this were true. And yet the truth of forgiveness as a means of grace is beyond denial: forgiving others frees *us* to be forgiven, and indeed, opens a path for others to know the wonderful, powerful love and acceptance of God in Jesus Christ our Lord.

Jesus' words to his disciples were clear regarding our duty to forgive:

> Then Peter came and said to him, "Lord, if another member of the church sins against me, how often should I forgive? As many as seven times?" Jesus said to him, "Not seven times, but, I tell you, seventy-seven times. For this reason the kingdom of heaven may be compared to a king who wished to settle accounts with his slaves. When he began the reckoning, one who owed him ten thousand talents was brought to him; and, as he could not pay, his lord ordered him to be sold, together with his wife and children and all his possessions, and payment to be made. So the slave fell on his knees before him, saying, 'Have patience with me, and I will pay you everything.' And out of pity for him, the lord of that slave released him and forgave him the debt. But that same slave, as he went out, came upon one of his fellow slaves who owed him a hundred denarii; and seizing him by the throat, he said, 'Pay what you owe.' Then his fellow slave fell down and pleaded with him, 'Have patience with me, and I will pay you.' But he refused; then he went and threw him into prison until he would pay the debt. When his fellow slaves saw what had happened, they were greatly distressed, and they went and reported to their lord all that had taken place. Then his lord

summoned him and said to him, 'You wicked slave! I forgave you all that debt because you pleaded with me. Should you not have had mercy on your fellow slave, as I had mercy on you?' And in anger his lord handed him over to be tortured until he would pay his entire debt. So my heavenly Father will also do to every one of you, if you do not forgive your brother or sister from your heart."[159]

This is a convicting passage. We are first told to continually forgive—seventy-seven times clearly means "always" and "forever"—and then we are given this parable to remind us of *why* we should forgive. Put simply, God is the King and we are the servant who was forgiven a debt far beyond our ability to repay. Because of the King's graciousness we stand forgiven; how can we *possibly* turn to our fellow servants in this life and demand repayment of the pittance that they owe us? The debts that others may owe us pale in comparison to the debt we owed, just as the debt of the second servant was insignificant compared to the debt that the first servant was forgiven. Rather than demanding payment, we should be overwhelmed with thanksgiving for the grace of the master and be eager to forgive these tiny debts that are owed to us. If we have learned *anything* about the nature of God's grace, this is *precisely* what we should do.

Unfortunately, most of us are not quick to forgive. Instead, we are frighteningly like the first servant who, although he was forgiven a huge debt, couldn't express the same grace to his fellow servant that was expressed to him by the King. We hold grudges. We hold debts. We hold the bruises of broken relationships and painful memories. We hold on to these debts and refuse to let go, acting as if they were precious to us. We hold the pain of these trespasses very close, guarding against the possibility that our anger and pain over debts owed to us might ebb away. Indeed, one might even go so far

---

[159]   Matthew 18:21-35

as to suspect that we love the pain of broken trust and destroyed relationships far more than we love the grace and peace that comes from holy reconciliation.

The sad truth is that, when we refuse to forgive, when we cling to the debts that others owe us, we are doing ourselves far more harm than anyone else. We can nurse a grudge and fuel our resentments, but when we do so we are the ones who are hurt. Why do we do this to ourselves? There are many reasons, but I suspect that a large part of our resistance to forgiving is fear of rejection and repeated injury. Frequently, we believe that if we forgive someone they will sense weakness in us and "do it to us again." While past experience may well substantiate such a fear, the truth is that we don't *really* know what will happen when we offer forgiveness. We can also be certain that, until we *do* forgive, we will be the only ones who will continue to be hurt.

"How often should I forgive?" The answer may not be at all comfortable, and yet we cannot ignore the words of our Lord: "Seventy-seven times." In other words, we should always be ready and willing to forgive those sins that have been committed against us.

Forgiving is not easy, and we all have bruises that linger from our past. For some, it's a friendship that has been destroyed by the betrayal of confidences. For others, that friendship was broken by lies, or damaged by neglect, or injured by abuse. Sometimes our pains are deeply felt and are difficult to root out. Other times they rest on the surface, and it becomes a simple matter to recognize our own participation in the destruction of relationships. However, no matter how difficult, or how deep, or how extensive our bruises may be, the path to healing always begins with forgiveness. Because we have been forgiven so very much, we *must* forgive.

The sacramental means of grace always entail a human response. Jesus died on the cross, once and for all, and on him *all* the sins of humanity were placed. However, unless and until we accept the offered gift, and unless we offer our forgiveness and the word of our Lord's forgiveness to others, *we* erect roadblocks to God's grace in our lives.

Jesus said to them again, "Peace be with you. As the Father has sent me, so I send you." When he had said this, he breathed on them and said to them, "Receive the Holy Spirit. If you forgive the sins of any, they are forgiven them; if you retain the sins of any, they are retained."[160]

This passage of scripture defines the root of our Christian authority in the forgiveness of sins. Jesus gives us the gift of the Holy Spirit, which makes it possible for us to forgive others, and then he sends us out into the world with a specific mission; we are called to forgive sins. This calling is an extension of the great commission. We proclaim the gospel of Jesus Christ, not just by telling others about his death and resurrection, but also by putting the effects of the cross into action by applying God's grace in reconciliation. It is our responsibility as a forgiven people to forgive others. Empowered by the Holy Spirit, and authorized by Scripture, we have access to this wonderful gift of grace; and we are called to offer that gift to others. When we offer our forgiveness and the forgiveness of our Lord Jesus Christ to others, we enter into the Apostolic calling to extend the love of God to a broken and hurting world. This world is filled with people who are in desperate need of hearing that God loves them. The famous words in the third chapter of John's Gospel have been repeated so frequently that they've almost become trite, and yet they are so very true:

For God so loved the world that he gave his only Son, so that everyone who believes in him may not perish but may have eternal life. Indeed, God did not send the Son into the world to condemn the world, but in order that the world might be saved through him.[161]

---

[160]   John 20:21-23
[161]   John 3:16-17

God doesn't hate the world, nor is God angry with the world or with us. God loves the world and loves each and every one of us, and earnestly desires us to live in a relationship with Jesus Christ. Indeed, that is why Jesus came into the world and died on the cross: so that, through his victory over sin and death, we could enter into a relationship with the divine Creator of the universe. God is for us, not against us, and desires to forgive us if only we will respond with faith to the offered gift by simply accepting it. This is the good news that we must share, and share in more than just words. Our calling is to share the gospel in words and in deeds, through what we say and by what we do. And when we forgive the sins of others, and in the name of Jesus forgive the sins of those who have sinned against God, we actualize the love of God for those who may have never heard of or known it.

The means of grace in forgiveness can open the way for the other means of grace to grow and flourish in our lives. As a means of grace, acts of reconciliation can break down the hard crust of anger and indifference, pain and fear that many have formed over their spiritual skins. Unfortunately, many Protestants tend to be afraid, or at least leery, of this means of grace due to the mistaken assumption that Protestants don't make confessions.

In my capacity as a pastor, and in response to sermons in which I encourage people to engage in "radical acts of forgiveness," I am frequently asked:

"I thought Methodists didn't make confessions."

That depends upon what is meant by "making one's confession." If one means that Methodists and other Protestants don't confess their sins to God, that impression is wrong. We most certainly *do* confess our sins to God! Indeed, among the Methodists there are several liturgies, both in the Hymnal and in the Book of Worship, which aid us in making congregational Confessions of Sin. If, on the other hand, one means that Protestants don't have the tradition of sitting down with a minister or other Christian and making a confession of sin, they are correct; that kind of a confessional is no longer a *formal* part of many Protestant traditions.

This doesn't mean, however, that such confessionals don't ever happen in Protestant Churches. In the Episcopal Church, for example, a rite for "The Reconciliation of a Penitent" can be found in the *Book of Common Prayer* in two forms, both of which are designed for use by a penitent sinner and a minister. In such confessional settings, the minister is present to hear and give "such counsel and encouragement as are needed and pronounces absolution."[162]

It should be noted that the minister's purpose is two-fold: firstly, the minister is there to listen as the confession is made so that he or she will be able to provide informed counsel concerning how the penitent may overcome the sinful tendencies, habits, or acts that have been confessed. In the past, when I have partaken of this rite, I have found the guidance of the minister quite helpful in discerning the source of my sinful tendencies, as well as in leading me in establishing which spiritual disciplines would be helpful in overcoming those tendencies. Secondly, the minister is there to offer the prayer of absolution over the penitent, a prayer which I have personally found to be a source of great comfort and which I have used with my own people when they have sought me out for such confessional rites:

> Our Lord Jesus Christ, who has left power to his Church to absolve all sinners who truly repent and believe in him, of his great mercy forgive you all your offenses; and by his authority committed to me, I absolve you from all your sins: in the Name of the Father, and of the Son, and of the Holy Spirit. *Amen.*[163]

---

[162] *Book of Common Prayer*, "Concerning the Rite," 446.
[163] ibid., 448.

While making a formal confession is not the traditional practice among United Methodists, over the past couple of decades in my ministry I have heard a surprisingly large number of private confessions. Sometimes it's helpful for us to go to someone we respect for their spiritual insight, tell them what we've done wrong, and seek advice on how to go about setting things right. That is a Confession of Sin, and it happens far more often than many Protestants could imagine!

Depending upon the religious background of those seeking help in making confession to God, I will often suggest one of the formal liturgies that exist among Protestants. For example, there are the before-mentioned rites found in the Episcopal Church's *Book of Common Prayer,* and there's the often-overlooked "Service of Healing II" found in *The United Methodist Book of Worship.*[164] This is an excellent liturgy intended for use in either private or corporate worship, and contains two confessional invitations that are particularly noteworthy:

> *Name,* the Scriptures tell us to bear
> > one another's burdens
> > and so fulfill the law of Christ.
> As your *sister/brother* in Christ, I ask you now,
> > are you at peace with God,
> > or is there anything in your life
> > that causes you to feel separated from God
> > and less than the full person
> > God calls you to be?

> *Name,* the Scriptures tell us not to be anxious
> > about our lives
> > or about tomorrow.
> Are there anxieties that cause you to feel separated
> > from the peace that God promises?[165]

---

[164] *The United Methodist Book of Worship,* 622–623.
[165] ibid.

Following either of these invitations, the penitent is invited to reflect in silence or to engage in a time of personal sharing with the pastor. After this time of frank conversation regarding the temptations and sins that are plaguing them, the service then recommends the use of one of the prayers of confession and pardon that can be found in *The Book of Worship* as well as in *The United Methodist Hymnal*. For an example, my favorite is #890 in the back of the *Hymnal*. This prayer, or one very similar to it, is currently in use by many denominations in corporate worship. Of particular note, it includes reference to both the sins of commission as well as the sins of omission—"what we have done" as well as "what we have left undone." In my own ministry, as well as in personal use, I have found it especially helpful to change the personal pronouns from the first-person plurals—"we," "us," and "ourselves"—to the first-person singulars—"I," "me," and "myself." When done, the prayer reads like this:

> Most merciful God,
> I confess that I have sinned against you
> in thought, word, and deed,
> by what I have done,
> and by what I have left undone.
> I have not loved you with my whole heart;
> I have not loved my neighbor as myself.
> I am truly sorry and I humbly repent.
> For the sake of your Son Jesus Christ,
> have mercy on me and forgive me;
> that I may delight in your will,
> and walk in your ways,
> to the glory of your name. Amen.[166]

In addition to changing the plural pronouns to singulars, this prayer can be personalized even further by inserting any specific sins that

---

[166]   UM *Hymnal*, 890, as adapted for use by an individual. See also *Book of Common Prayer*, 360.

one might wish to give over to God. They can be placed nearly anywhere, but they are most easily placed following the words: "I have not loved my neighbor as myself."

There are times when sins are easy to relinquish, but there are other times when, for whatever reason, we don't want to give up to Jesus the sins we have committed. Sometimes, by simply voicing such sins we can find the grace we need to truly let go of the guilt that plagues us and receive the forgiveness of God. It is an awesome experience to kneel before God and make a confession like this, and it is equally powerful to hear the words of absolution:

> Almighty God have mercy on you,
> forgive all your sins through our Lord Jesus Christ,
> strengthen you in all goodness,
> and by the power of the Holy Spirit
> keep you in eternal life.[167]

These words of assurance can bring hope and healing. For a person who is seeking forgiveness, they can aid in knowing the love and acceptance of Jesus Christ. But, truth be told, the experience of hearing them is not for everyone. The objection is sometimes voiced:

"I don't need anyone between me and Jesus!"

And this is certainly true. Theologically speaking, there *is* no one between the penitent and Jesus. Even when one makes one's confession of sin with a minister present, the minister is powerless apart from the Word of God. One makes one's confession of sin to Jesus; the minister is there to give counsel and advice, and to pronounce the words: "In the Name of Jesus Christ, your sins are forgiven."

---

[167] ibid.

Healing

Are any among you sick? They should call for the elders
of the church and have them pray over them,
anointing them with oil in the name of the Lord.
—*James 5:13-15*

Evelyn was a dear woman. Every time I visited her it was always a joy to be greeted by her smile, her warm embrace, and her gentle laugh. Of all the elderly shut-ins whom I visited on a regular basis, she was the one whom I always looked forward to seeing. Visiting her wasn't a chore, nor was it depressing. She always had a happy, positive, expansive outlook on life and the future, and never gave in to the depression, self-pity, or bitterness that would be understandable given her condition.

You see, for many years Evelyn suffered from the painful ravages of cancer. Breast cancer, lung cancer, bone marrow cancer ... no sooner had she beaten down a malignancy in one area of her body than another would rear its ugly head elsewhere. Long before I met her, and long before she had become too ill to get out and come to church on a regular basis, Evelyn's life had become one long, continuous battle with a body which was rebelling against her life. Just about anyone else might have given up long before, but not Evelyn. No, for this woman of powerful faith, each and every day of struggle had become yet another opportunity for expressing the love of God.

I'll never forget the day when she went into the hospital for her last intensive round of radical chemotherapy. I knew she was dreading it, but she *never* let on how afraid she was. In the past the chemotherapy treatments had been harsh; this promised to be the worst yet. Be that as it may, when I saw Evelyn her eyes were bright and her smile was broad and *real*. I remember sitting down next to her, taking her hand, and spending a wonderful half-hour just waiting for them to come and give her the treatment. Toward the end of our conversation she got quiet, looked directly at me, and said, "Let's pray." And then, rather than waiting for me to begin, she opened her own mouth and began to offer up her words to God. She prayed for her doctors, her nurses, her family, her friends, and for me. She prayed for everyone, everyone but herself.

I couldn't stand it. I began to cry as she prayed; and as I listened to the deep concern that she had for everyone else, I grew to comprehend the grace that she had been given. It was beautiful; it also gave me a little bit of an insight into how she had managed to hold up under the constant stress and strain of being ill for so long. Rather than obsessing upon her own pain, her own fears, and her own sickness, she focused upon the needs and concerns of others. She didn't ignore her own condition; rather, she was more concerned with how *other* people dealt with her condition.

As she fell silent, I began to croak out a prayer for her. I felt so inadequate, but I prayed that Jesus would be with her, touch her, and heal her. I took out a vial of oil, made the sign of the cross on her forehead, and then closed off my prayer for her by thanking God for the powerful grace of Jesus Christ that God had honored me to see in her. I then gave her a hug and she, smiling up at me, said, "That was beautiful, honey, but Jesus has already healed me. This cancer …it's annoying, and it hurts, and I'd like to be cured, but I'm already *healed*."

With tears flowing, all I could say was "Praise God."

Evelyn was *cured* a few weeks later when Jesus took her home to be with him in heaven. But Evelyn was right: *long* before she was cured, she had been healed. Long before her physical suffering had come to an end, God had healed her.

It is easy to become caught up in the conditions of life. It is easy to focus upon our illnesses and the immediacy of our pains and discomforts. This is only natural; when I am sick, *all* I want is to be made well. I can wax long and rhapsodic on the virtues of healing that exist above and beyond the physical manifestations, but when I'm sick I really want to be cured. Indeed, no one can be blamed for wanting to be cured of an illness; no one likes being sick. However, we can be so narrowly focused upon physical curing that we rarely remember that healing is far more than just a physical phenomenon. It includes, but is not limited to, physical curing.

To be healed means to be made whole. It means to be made complete. It means to be made at peace with God, with creation, and with oneself. Healing is the re-establishment of a right relationship with God, a relationship for which we were made and from which we have strayed in our sins and our unwillingness to remain open to the love and presence of God in our lives. As Martin Israel, physician and Episcopal priest, writes in his book *Healing as Sacrament:*

> Healing is not a patchwork repair; it is a re-creation of something that has strayed from the image that God originally conceived.[168]

We were created to live in a relationship with God, and part of our susceptibility to illness follows from our inability to live according to God's will within this relationship. We think we know what is always right for us, and so we end up abusing our bodies and our minds and our spirits through overwork, overeating, overstressing, and under-maintenance. Part of being made whole is being returned to the relationship that we are called to have with God. This return, this "re-creation" of the image of God in us, does include the curing of physical, emotional, and mental illnesses; but curing is not all that there is to healing. And that is, quite frankly, one of the most difficult aspects of the sacramental means of grace in healing.

"If God promises to heal me, why am I not healed?"

Few questions are more painful to hear, and more difficult to answer, than this one. If we are healed, and that healing is sure and certain,

---

168   Martin Israel, *Healing as Sacrament* (Cambridge: Cowley Publications, 1984), 8.

than why don't we always see the outward physical manifestation of that healing? In other words, why don't we experience "curing" along with "healing?" True, sometimes we do, but often the reality of our healing runs far deeper than just our physical experience would indicate. Sometimes the healing that we really need is not so much physical as it is spiritual. Granted, this is not easy for anyone to hear, and yet it is a reality which we all must eventually face. Indeed, it was a reality that my friend Evelyn faced, and accepted, with faith, hope, and love on her lips and in her heart. Evelyn knew that her healing was real, and present, and that it involved her being made "whole" and at peace. For Evelyn, being healed meant being with God—healing was being delivered, restored, and saved.

In the Greek New Testament the word that is usually translated into English as "saved" is "sozo":

$$\sigma\acute{\omega}\zeta\omega$$

As is the case with many Greek words, it contains several different, yet related, connotations. It means to preserve, rescue, deliver, save, bring to safety, and bring to wholeness.[169] It is sometimes used in the New Testament for healing, as in the ninth chapter of Matthew where Jesus heals the woman who had been suffering from hemorrhages for twelve years:

> Jesus turned, and seeing her he said, "Take heart, daughter; your faith has made you well." And instantly the woman was made well.[170]

---

[169]   W. Foerster, σώζω TDNT 7:990–991.
[170]   Matthew 9:22

The word rendered "well" in the *NRSV* translates a Greek formation of σώζω.[171] While some might want to translate this as "saved," the context is one of a healing and not justification.[172] And, yet, that's the whole point: salvation and healing are two sides of the same coin. Being made whole, or healed, is as much a spiritual event as it is a physical one. When we are saved, we are healed; when we are healed, we are also saved. Christ's self-giving sacrifice brings delivery from both temporal and eternal suffering. This is properly the role of the suffering servant.

Ever since the early days of the Church, Christians have looked to the Old Testament to provide them with an interpretation of the suffering and death of Jesus. After all, the Jewish concept of the Messiah didn't include the idea of his suffering and dying. The Messiah was supposed to be victorious over the powers and forces of evil in the world—he wasn't supposed to be killed by them! Hence, early Christians were faced with a serious dilemma: they were still Jews, and yet they followed a Messiah who had died! How were they going to deal with this serious inconsistency?

They found their answer in the pages of the prophet Isaiah, and specifically in the concept of the "Suffering Servant." While the nominal Jewish interpretation didn't view the Suffering Servant motif as being fulfilled in an individual person, and they certainly didn't connect this person with the Messiah, Christians found in this concept a key to unlocking the theological significance of the suffering and death of Jesus. The passage of critical importance is found in Isaiah's fifty-third chapter:

> Surely he hath borne our griefs, and carried our
> sorrows: yet we did esteem him stricken, smitten
> of God, and afflicted. But he was wounded for our

---

[171]   σέσωκέν, which is the 3rd singular, present active indicative formation of σώζω.
[172]   The *NRSV, NASB, ESV, AMP, CEV, TEV, HCSB,* and *The Message* all render it as "well." The *NIV* and *REB* both render it as "healed." The *KJV, Geneva,* and *Douay* all render it as "whole." The *NJB* renders it as "saved."

transgressions, he was bruised for our iniquities: the chastisement of our peace was upon him; and with his stripes we are healed.[173]

Through the centuries, Christians have found in this passage a powerful theological interpretation of the suffering and death of Jesus. This interpretation has two important aspects, both of which touch upon healing.

Firstly, it says that Jesus was "wounded for our transgressions" and "bruised for our iniquities." In these words we find a direct connection between our sins and Jesus' sufferings. Christians proclaim that Jesus came to take the sins of the world upon himself and then to end the division between God and humankind by dying in our place. This is known as the doctrine of the Substitutionary Atonement. This understanding of the suffering and death of Jesus is never properly spoken of without reflecting upon the love of God, which can be comprehended in our Lord's death for our sins.

We can't heal the rift that we have torn between God and ourselves, so God did it by giving himself up *for* us. In the death of Jesus on the cross, we are reminded that God loves us so much that he is willing to stand in our place. He actually *has* faced death for us. In that holy moment upon the cross, when he died, all the sins of the world—past, present, and future—were paid for. Nothing more needs to be done to pay for them or to break down the wall of separation between us and God. However, just because our sins are paid for doesn't mean that the gift has been received and applied on our behalf. We have the responsibility of responding to God's offered grace with faith. Then, and only then, are we saved.

Functioning from within the context of forgiveness, we find that divine healing is also referenced in the Isaiah passage: "and by his stripes, we are healed." Our Lord's "stripes" were the places in his flesh where he was whipped to the point that his blood flowed.

---

[173]   Isaiah 53:4-5 *KJV*

Our sicknesses are like his stripes: our life flows out through our illnesses and the ravages of sickness beat us up. In and through Jesus' sufferings, he was beaten by life and death *for* us and in our place.

Both salvation and healing come when we accept the gift Christ offers. And what is healing? Sometimes it is physical, sometimes emotional, sometimes spiritual, and sometimes relational. Sometimes we know healing here on Earth in the form of curing, and sometimes we must wait for the cure in glory while nevertheless experiencing true wholeness and the peace of being delivered to the embrace of God.

Which brings us back to our earlier question:

"If God promises to heal me, why am I not healed?"

Put another way: why isn't everyone healed, visibly, here on this Earth? That is a difficult question. Suffice it to say that no one should *ever* allow anyone to say that they're not cured because they don't have faith. Few things make me angrier than the guilt-trip that some want to place on those who are not always and immediately cured! Physical healing *may* come in this life, but it's not a lack of faith that causes some people to not be cured in the here and now. The promise, and God's grace, is still ready and available for any and all to receive; and healing *does* occur, even if it's not seen in one's physical life. The healing may not be manifested until we enter glory, or it may be manifested in ways that we least expect—emotional and spiritual rather than physical—but the promise is sure and true and we can depend upon it. We should give thanks to God that the healing grace of Jesus is present to make us whole again. That is the true essence of healing; it's not just the mending of broken bodies, it's the "making whole" of lives that have been torn asunder by being separated from God.

The Body of Christ is authorized to proclaim healing in Jesus' name. Just as we have been called by Christ to forgive the sins of any who come seeking forgiveness, so also we are called to offer the healing grace of our Savior to the last, the least, and the lost. We are called to extend the hand of peace and to proclaim the reconciling love of our Savior to the whole world. Even if we fear that there may not be a "cure" to be seen in any given circumstance or instance, we are still called to proclaim healing. Scripture is clear:

> Are any among you sick? They should call for the elders of the church and have them pray over them, anointing them with oil in the name of the Lord. The prayer of faith will save the sick, and the Lord will raise them up; and anyone who has committed sins will be forgiven. Therefore confess your sins to one another, and pray for one another, so that you may be healed. The prayer of the righteous is powerful and effective.[174]

The gift of divine healing is seated in the grace of God, active in the community of faith and functioning through prayer. All those who offer their prayers to God are granted the wonderful privilege of participating in the healing actions of God's grace. The gift of healing is fundamentally part of the ministry of the Body of Christ, carried forward by all believers and by the leaders of the community. Due to the clear link between healing and forgiveness found in Scripture, we also believe that healing is an extension of the wonderful gift of our Lord's death on the cross.

When it comes to healing and forgiveness, sometimes we have a problem accepting that God has really given himself for us and accepts us regardless of what we do. We want to rip the sins off of our Lord, which he bore on the cross for us, and put them on our own backs. We want to take back our illnesses and act as if God can't or won't heal us. We deny the gift of forgiveness, and the healing power that the gift brings; and we try to take back the sins and the

---

[174]   James 5:14-16

infirmities that Christ has long ago died for. This is actually a form of sin, for it is a direct denial of God's desire to give us his powerful grace. Jesus offers us so much in his grace, and it begins with the healing that comes in forgiveness!

Evelyn knew that she was healed. She knew it *long* before she entered the hospital for her last chemotherapy treatments. Even though she wasn't cured, she knew that through the grace of God she had been "made whole." For her, the reality of having been healed was just as certain as the reality of her salvation. Indeed, as we have seen through the insight that we have gained from Isaiah 53, forgiveness and healing really go hand in hand as a blessing to all of God's children.

Marriage

> On the third day there was a wedding in Cana of Galilee, and the mother of Jesus was there. Jesus and his disciples had also been invited to the wedding.
> —*John 2:1-2*

My parents had an incredible marriage. I know I'm biased, but in my opinion theirs was a partnership which provided mutual support, love, and companionship for them and for their children and grandchildren. No marriage can be perfect, and yet my parents managed to form and live in one that was as close to perfect as could be imagined. This doesn't mean that they didn't have difficult times, or that there weren't occasions when their marriage teetered on the edge of oblivion. What it does mean is that they found ways to make their marriage work, ways that depended upon love: the love they had for each other, for their children, and for God. Fundamentally, their marriage worked because it depended upon the grace of Jesus Christ. And it was that grace which held them together even through the long days of sickness and pain which preceded my Dad's death.

I once asked Mother to list those things which made their marriage work so well for more than half a century. The list that she produced could have gone on for many pages, but among those things that she gave me were the following important factors:

- Patience: for self and the other.
- Caring: for the needs and concerns of the other.
- Learning: about the other and about self.
- Prayer: for each other and the family.
- Understanding: for the humanness of the other.
- Love: for God and the other.
- And the Lord, above all else, in the middle.

In fact, upon reflection my mother has affirmed that, if it were not for the presence of God's love and grace in the midst of their marriage, they would not have remained together until the end. Their marriage was sacramental in nature because it depended upon the grace of the Lord Jesus Christ for its existence and growth. Because of God's grace, their marriage was transformative for the lives of those who shared it and who were touched by it.

Dad's thoughts upon their marriage can best be summarized with his following word-picture:

> A marriage is like a collection of automobile parts. One can collect together all the parts that go into making up a car: the engine, the frame, the doors and windows, the electrical system, the fuel tank and the fuel, the wheels, the lights, and the upholstered seats. All these parts can be piled up on your garage floor, and you can even stand back and say "my, what a beautiful car!" And in some respects, you'll be right— the parts for a beautiful automobile are sitting, piled up, on the floor of your garage. But when you put the key into the ignition switch and turn it, what happens?

Nothing. While all the needed parts may be gathered together in one place on the floor of your garage, until they've been put together in a precise way you don't have a car. It takes someone with intelligence, with an understanding of how automobiles are put together, to come along and actually assemble all the various parts. Until they're put together, a collection of automobile parts won't carry you one inch; but once they've been assembled, they become more than the sum of their parts … they become a car that can carry you a hundred thousand miles. A marriage is like that; it is more than the sum of its parts. A marriage works when its parts come together, under the guidance of the Maker, to create a new whole. Until then, it's just a jumbled up collection of spare parts.

My father was right. A marriage is more than just the coming together of two individuals. A marriage is the unique *union* of two souls, following the guidance and plan of the Maker, and as such we say that a marriage is a means of grace. Just as a dictionary isn't any more one of Shakespeare's plays just because it contains all the words that one will find in such a play, so also a car isn't a car or a marriage isn't a marriage unless the parts are properly assembled. And that is what God's grace in Christian marriage is all about.

Jesus was present for at least one wedding—the one at Cana of Galilee, where he performed his first public miracle by changing water into wine; however, there is no indication anywhere within scripture that Jesus himself was married. Likewise, nowhere do we find Jesus establishing marriage as a sacrament. Our sisters and brothers in the Roman Catholic Church disagree with this conclusion. The *Catechism* of the Roman Catholic Church has this to say about marriage:

> The matrimonial covenant, by which a man and a woman establish between themselves a partnership of the whole of life, is by its nature ordered toward the good of the spouses and the procreation and education of offspring; this covenant between baptized persons has been raised by Christ the Lord to the dignity of a sacrament.[175]

There are many elements in this statement with which most Protestants can easily agree. We affirm that marriage establishes a partnership, which involves the whole life of those involved. We affirm that it is established for the good of those who are in it, and that it is within the marriage covenant that children are ideally reared and educated. We view it as a covenant relationship, and as a means of grace for those who enter into it; but we do not view it as a sacrament of the same order of magnitude as Holy Communion or Baptism. Specifically, we don't accept marriage as a sacrament because we cannot confirm through scripture that Jesus established it as such.

Our sisters and brothers in the Roman Catholic Church believe that our Lord's presence at the marriage in Cana constitutes such an establishment, but Protestants usually don't agree with this assessment. Likewise, Catholics affirm that the references to marriage in the Epistle to the Ephesians establish it as a sacrament:

> Wives, be subject to your husbands as you are to the Lord. For the husband is the head of the wife just as Christ is the head of the church, the body of which he is the Savior. Just as the church is subject to Christ, so also wives ought to be, in everything, to their husbands. Husbands, love your wives, just as Christ loved the church and gave himself up for her, in order to make her holy by cleansing her with

---

[175]   Roman *Catechism*, 400.

the washing of water by the word, so as to present the church to himself in splendor, without a spot or wrinkle or anything of the kind—yes, so that she may be holy and without blemish. In the same way, husbands should love their wives as they do their own bodies. He who loves his wife loves himself. For no one ever hates his own body, but he nourishes and tenderly cares for it, just as Christ does for the church, because we are members of his body. "For this reason a man will leave his father and mother and be joined to his wife, and the two will become one flesh." This is a great mystery, and I am applying it to Christ and the church.[176]

This statement, traditionally attributed to Paul but actually being of questionable authenticity,[177] affirms a relationship of special character between husband and wife—one that reflects the relationship between Christ and the church. Unfortunately, this is an often-misused passage. It is frequently cited to justify the subjection of women to the absolute, sometimes abusive, often arbitrary, authority of men without regard for the reciprocal nature of the relationship. Usually ignored is the phrase, "Husbands, love your wives, just as Christ loved the church and gave himself up for her…"[178]

Jesus doesn't get drunk and beat on the church or otherwise mistreat or cheat on the church. Jesus doesn't yell at the church, emotionally abuse the church, ignore the church, neglect the needs of the church, abandon the church, or in any way fail to care for the church. Hence, when husbands do such things to their wives, their wives aren't bound to accept it. These husbands have violated the covenant because such abuse is *not* in keeping with the witness

---

[176]   Ephesians 5:25–32
[177]   There are excellent arguments against the authenticity of the Letter to the Ephesians: it appears to be a collection of quotes from the other letters of Paul, compiled by a later editor.
[178]   Ephesians 5:25. See also Colossians 3:19, from whence the Ephesians verse is probably derived.

of Christ and the character of his self-giving love. Jesus died for the church; he doesn't abuse the church. Hence, when a husband disregards, ignores, mistreats, abuses, or otherwise violates the boundaries of the marriage covenant, the wife need not recognize or accept his authority.

As true as all of this is, it should also be noted that the conventional rendering of Ephesians 5:22, instructing wives to "be subject to" or "submit to" their husbands, is *highly questionable*. The most ancient surviving manuscript copies of Paul's letters—including 𝔓46 and Codex *Vaticanus*, among others—lack the Greek word for "submission" in Ephesians 5:22. Instead, the earliest best witnesses to the Greek text would probably be best translated as "be with" or, possibly, "exclusively to".[179] While the directive is still patriarchal, depending upon a different culture's standards for gender relations, nevertheless the principle being communicated is not so much one of raw authority as it is of fidelity. Essentially, the marriage covenant is a holy relationship; it isn't license for one member of the relationship to abuse the other but, rather, for fidelity and—in our context—for mutual support.

While Protestants don't consider marriage to be a sacrament, nevertheless we do recognize that marriage has many sacramental qualities and is, indeed, a means of grace. Through the rite of Christian Marriage a couple is joined together in a covenantal relationship with each other and with God. Through this covenant, two people commit themselves "to have and to hold, from this day forward, for better, for worse, for richer, for poorer, in sickness and in health, to love and to cherish..." until they are parted by death.[180] Prayed over such a couple are the following, powerful words:

---

[179] See the textual apparatus for Ephesians 5:22 in the *Nestle-Aland Novum Testamentum Graece*, 27th Edition (Stuttgart: Deutsche Bibelgesellschaft, 1991). See also Bruce M. Metzger, *A Textual Commentary of the Greek New Testament* (Stuttgart: United Bible Societies, 1975), 608–609.

[180] UM *Book of Worship*, 122–123.

> O God, you have so consecrated the covenant of
> Christian marriage that in it is represented the
> covenant between Christ and his Church. Send
> therefore your blessing upon *Name* and *Name* that
> they may surely keep their marriage covenant and so
> grow in love and godliness together that their home
> may be a haven of blessing and peace; through Jesus
> Christ our Lord. Amen.[181]

As a means of grace, marriage is a wonderful gift of God's love to the whole Body of Christ. As a means of grace containing sacramental characteristics, the institution of marriage is also a wonderful gift to Christian couples. It does not establish a relationship in which one member is made to obey the will of the other; rather, it establishes a covenant of mutual love, support, and respect in which two people join together to face life as one. This relationship of mutual love is empowered by the Holy Spirit and should exemplify the love of God, in Jesus Christ, for the church.

Ordination

Do not neglect the gift that is in you, which was given to you through prophecy
with the laying on of hands by the council of elders.
—1 Timothy 4:14

When I first answered the call to enter the ministry I never expected that being ordained would be a frightening experience. After all, it was a goal I had been working toward for many years. I had completed all of the educational requirements, had appeared before committee after committee, been asked dozens of theological questions, and had been required to write a lengthy paper on still

---

[181]   ibid.

more theological questions. I had been interviewed by several psychologists, psychiatrists, clergy, and theologians; and after many years of much hard work and study, I had been approved for ordination. It was the culmination of many dreams and prayers, and I was excited. So, why was I also so very scared?

I stood there with my fellow candidates as the Bishop examined us yet again. In The United Methodist Church candidates for ordination are questioned at several stages, the last being just before they are actually ordained. Some of the questions are quite difficult and require much consideration before a response can be made, while some are rather mundane and easy to answer. Among those final questions that are asked by the Bishop just before ordination, the following stand out:

- Are you persuaded that the scriptures of the Old and New Testaments contain all things necessary for salvation through faith in Jesus Christ, and are the unique and authoritative standard for the Church's faith and life?
- Will you be faithful in prayer, in the reading and study of the Holy Scriptures, and with the help of the Holy Spirit continually rekindle the gift of God that is in you?
- Will you be a steadfast disciple of Christ, so that your life may be fashioned by the gospel, and provide a faithful example for all God's people?
- In covenant with other elders, will you be loyal to The United Methodist Church, accepting its order, liturgy, doctrine, and discipline, defending it against all doctrines contrary to God's Holy Word, and accepting the authority of those who are appointed to supervise your ministry?[182]

I would suspect that these questions would present at least a little difficulty for many Christians—not just clergy, and not just United

---

[182]   All from, UM *Book of Worship*, 675–676.

Methodists. Let's take a few moments to consider each of them in turn.

Do we *truly* believe that the scriptures "are the unique and authoritative standard"[183] for our Christian faith and living? Given the perennial debates in The United Methodist Church over the issue of authority, I have to ask this question with more than just a little bit of incredulity; indeed, the same question could easily be asked of Christians in many different denominations. Do we *really* believe that the Scriptures have authority for our faith and living? Do we truly turn to the Bible for guidance, or do we believe we can just jettison it when and where it becomes too difficult for us to consider honestly?

The second question is just as difficult, for it is so easy to neglect the wonderful gift of grace that we have received. We are frequently tempted to disregard the gift of the Holy Spirit, who comes to live within us in our baptisms and, if ordained, also through the laying on of hands. Neglect of the spiritual disciplines, of prayer and scriptural study, can be so very tempting and easy to rationalize in the face of the duties, responsibilities, and pressures of "life here and now." How many times have I said: "visiting Evelyn is more important than studying the Bible"? Indeed, visiting "Evelyn" *is* very important—please don't misunderstand me—but so is scriptural study. My error, and the error of so many, is in believing and behaving as if these duties were in conflict. They are not. Indeed, they each support the other. Upon reflection, I've found that I've slipped into the deepest, darkest valleys of my life when I have failed to partake of the means of grace—means like prayer and scriptural study.

Likewise, the third question is difficult because when prayer and Scripture cease to become central in my spiritual life my discipleship suffers. This was true when I was a layperson, and it has been proven to be even more so in my pastoral ministry. It's been true for Christian clergy in many different denominations, and I believe it may even be

---

[183]   ibid.

a universal observation. When we neglect the means of grace that our Lord has given us, we are doomed to failure. When we ignore the grace of Jesus, and pretend as though we can "make it" on our own, we disconnect ourselves from the source of our strength. Is it any wonder that our spirituality frequently ends up wrecked on the shoals of life?

Which brings us to the last question. This one is so very hard because it can be difficult to be loyal to a community of faith that is made up of failing human beings—people who, like myself, sometimes go their own way, following their own wills and not God's will. When I see God's grace being denied, intolerance and bigotry being practiced and preached, hate and anger and separation being championed, I find it very hard to subject myself to the authority of those whom God has placed over me. And yet, when I answered this question with: "I will, with the help of God," I committed myself, of my own free will, to the grace of God and submitted myself to the authority of the church. Many clergy are tempted to take this "yoke of obedience" far too lightly, just as many of the laity are tempted to take lightly the obligations of church membership. And yet, we dare *not* take any of these commitments lightly.

The good news is that we are not expected to keep these words by ourselves. We are graced with the presence of the Holy Spirit, who enables us to be faithful. This gift of the divine presence is precisely what we mean when we refer to ordination as a means of grace.

My mind was swirling around with these questions while I waited to be called up into the chancel. And, when my name was finally called, and I was led up by my sponsoring Elders and directed to kneel before the Bishop, I discovered that I had developed a severe case of the shakes. I was half-expecting someone to stand up in the rear of the sanctuary and shout: "I know something about this yay-hoo that you don't know ... don't ordain him!" I had a horrible case of "imposteritis," for I knew how disastrously I fell short of deserving what was about to be given to me. With my mind, I knew that ordination was a wonderful expression of God's grace, but I couldn't shake the deeply seated feeling that I was the wrong person for this calling.

I knew that this feeling wasn't unique to me; abject inadequacy in the face of God's calling is common, with many Biblical examples to remind us that God has frequently called on those who knew how unworthy, and how much in need of God's grace, they actually were. Remember Moses? He repeatedly tried to find loopholes to get out of God's calling, finally whining:

> "O my Lord, I have never been eloquent, neither in the past nor even now that you have spoken to your servant; but I am slow of speech and slow of tongue."[184]

These could have easily been my own words, and I distinctly remember saying similar things to God prior to my ordination. After all, I was still frequently nervous when speaking in front of large groups of people. When I was a child I had struggled with stuttering. I don't have a legacy of clergy in my family, leading the way for me; I'm the first pastor in my family in nearly a century! "Oh God, you can't be calling me to the ordained ministry! Don't you mean to choose someone else?" Try as I might, my questions and self-doubts didn't win-out over the inner sense of call that continued to draw me into the service of God. Even with the fear, even with the questions, and even with the "imposteritis," I still knelt and waited for the Bishop, joined by the other Elders, to lay his hands on my head.

Ordination is a high holy moment that brings with it many life-changing implications. It's not just a licensing, nor is it just the recognition of something that God has already done; it is an actualizing of a gift of God's grace. Ordination is the "putting into effect" of a mission and ministry that comes from God and is recognized by the Church. Ordination is the "setting-apart" of one

---

[184]   Exodus 3:10

whom God has chosen to represent the Divine to the people and the people to the Divine. Those who are ordained carry with them the realization that *something* has happened to them. According to Dennis Campbell:

> Ordination marks us for life. This marking is not a life-long indelible character change, but it is a permanently significant reality. The church perceives the ordained person as different and so does the world. Sometimes this marking is recognized and expressed in simple ways such as the effort to "clean up the language around the preacher," or the perception that even if one enters another vocation and ceases to serve the church as a pastor, one is "different" for having once been a minister... The reason for this is that the idea of ordination is to "set apart." Rightly understood, ordination involves commitment freely to relinquish the self in order to become servant of the church. The self-relinquishing reality of ordination includes the matter of identity. The identity of the ordained is permanently linked to the identity of the church.[185]

This is true for the baptized as well: the identity of the baptized is linked to the identity of the church, for in a fundamental sense the baptized *are* the church. All Christians are called and ordained, in their baptisms, to ministry in the church. All Christians are part of the "Priesthood of Believers" and are called to reach out to others with the gospel of Jesus Christ. However, some of those who are baptized are further "set apart" for the representative pastoral ministries of "Service, Word, Sacrament, and Order." While Protestants don't recognize ordination as a sacrament, we nevertheless view it as

---

[185]   Dennis M. Campbell, *The Yoke of Obedience: The Meaning of Ordination in Methodism* (Nashville: Abingdon Press, 1989), 95–96.

having serious sacramental qualities. Ordination is a means of grace through which those who are called to ordained ministry are granted the divine assistance—the real presence of Jesus—which they need to serve and lead God's people, proclaim the gospel, and celebrate the sacraments.

This grace was given to me in 1994 when I was ordained to the Presbyterate of The United Methodist Church. Bishop Bruce Blake laid his hands on my head and prayed:

> Lord, pour upon Gregory Scott Neal the Holy Spirit, for the office and work of an elder, in the name of the Father, and of the Son, and of the Holy Spirit.
>
> Greg, take authority as an elder in the Church to preach the Word of God, and to administer the Holy Sacraments.[186]

Wow! When I think back upon this event the emotions of awe, fear, and excitement all surface with full force. In that moment of overwhelming grace, I became keenly aware that Jesus was kneeling there with me, as well as through the Bishop laying his hands upon me and praying for me. It was most certainly a means of grace. In that moment, God's unmerited favor was poured out upon me; and I received what I will always need, every day, to carry forward the ministry of Jesus Christ in the Church. Truly, it is a wonderful gift!

---

[186]   UM *Book of Worship*, 677–678. The UMC's Ordinal has been updated in recent years to reflect the changes that have been made to our Orders of Ministry.

Prayer

> Rejoice in hope, be patient in suffering, persevere in prayer.
> *—Romans 12:12*

One recurrent theme throughout all the means of grace, and one which we have seen to be of particular importance for the sacraments and the sacramentals, has been the importance of prayer in the Christian life. Indeed, in and through both individual and corporate prayer we are brought into a closer, more meaningful, and eternally abiding relationship with God. In many respects, prayer is the medium, the forum, and the substance through which the means of grace function. Prayer is a means of grace; it is also a component of the other means of grace. This means that prayer is utterly indispensable for the Christian life. Show me a Christian who doesn't pray, and I'll show you someone who isn't a Christian.

Unfortunately, among many Christians today there is much misunderstanding regarding what prayer actually *is*. We certainly don't treat prayer as if it were communication with God. I invite you to think honestly for a moment about what you do in your prayer life. How much of your time do you spend in an active mode while you pray, and how much time do you spend listening for God's part of the conversation? And, how do you go about listening?

Let's be honest. Usually, we come to God with a whole laundry list of needs, cares, and concerns, as well as with a collection of preconceptions concerning God's will for us at any given point in our lives. Thinking that we know what we need to be praying for, we kneel down and throw ourselves into our prayers without much concern for the nature of prayer as a conversation *with*, and not a monologue *to*, God. We talk our heads off telling God who, what, and how wonderful God is, as well as all of our desires for our life with Jesus, the forgiveness of our sins, and the salvation of other people's souls. We frequently spend several minutes telling God all sorts of things that God already knows; indeed, we sometimes even sound as

if we're preaching a sermon to God! After we've told God all about
the gospel, about how Jesus came into the world to save sinners,
and about how much we love him for having died for our sins, we
then begin begging God for all sorts of things. I'm reminded of the
wonderful scriptural passage:

> Again, truly I tell you, if two of you agree on earth
> about anything you ask, it will be done for you by my
> Father in heaven.[187]

There are times when it would appear that we not only think of this
passage literally, but we try to enact it in materialistic ways as well.
I've even seen sincere, faithful, otherwise sane Christians pray for
Lincoln Town Cars, fully expecting that one would be given to them
simply because they'd prayed for it! Thankfully, most of the time
our prayers are for things and circumstances, needs and concerns
that are far more reasonable, and appropriate, than new cars or other
adult "toys."

Please don't misunderstand: making petition to God for our needs,
for the needs of our loved ones, and for the needs and concerns of our
community, is *very* appropriate. Unfortunately, sometimes we treat
prayer as if it were begging. Yes, I've done my own share of begging
at the altar of the Lord, and I must say that God's grace has given
me truly what God knew I needed. Sometimes what I needed was
not what I thought I needed, or even what I was praying for; but in
retrospect, it's obvious that God knew what God was doing! Issuing
our petitions to God isn't all that prayer is about; neither is prayer
engaging in a monologue. Sadly, a lot of the time we don't do much
more than offer a lengthy monologue, then say "Amen," and get up
and go on about our business. We ignore God.

Prayer isn't just our talking to God; it is also—at least as
importantly—our listening for the voice of God in our lives. We can

---

[187]   Matthew 18:19

hear God speak to us in many different ways: through Scripture; through the words of great Christian authors, poets, song and hymn writers; through the words of our family, friends, and loved ones; and, even through that still-small-voice deep down inside us. There are many ways of hearing the voice of God. Prayer is about opening oneself to that voice and allowing God to speak to us, wherever we are and whatever our needs may be.

Sometimes we get so super-spiritual about prayer that we miss the radical reality of its dynamic presence in our lives. We are called to pray everywhere, all the time, and not just at Church or in private.

> Rejoice in the Lord always; again I will say, Rejoice.
> Let your gentleness be known to everyone. The Lord is
> near. Do not worry about anything, but in everything
> by prayer and supplication with thanksgiving let your
> requests be made known to God. And the peace of
> God, which surpasses all understanding, will guard
> your hearts and your minds in Christ Jesus.[188]

In our prayer life we are called to "rejoice in the Lord always." Even though we live in a difficult world, and even though our lives are very full and fast-paced, we can know the true peace of the presence of Jesus Christ in our lives if we will only open ourselves to him in prayer. That is how we, as a people of faith, can overcome such horrible tragedies like the shooting of children in high schools or the deaths of family, friends, and loved ones from illness or natural disaster. Left to our own strength, abilities, and resources, we will surely fail to persevere through the tragedies that this life can throw at us. But, with the strength, power, and love of Almighty God, working in and through us—through the many wonderful means of God's grace—we can be assured of the strength and the peace to make it through our trials and tribulations.

---

[188] Philippians 4:4–7

Did you notice what Paul did *not* say? He didn't say, "Come to Jesus and you'll never again have any problems!" No, the Apostle wrote: "do not worry about anything, but in everything by prayer and supplication with thanksgiving let your requests be made known to God." The implication is obvious—bad things *will* happen; they always have and, in this life, they *always* will. But through prayer, through abiding in the love of God in Jesus Christ, we can be assured that we will have the peace of God which passes all of our human ways of understanding.

Giving

> A woman came to [Jesus] with an alabaster jar of very costly ointment,
> and she poured it on his head as he sat at the table. But when the disciples
> saw it, they were angry and said, "Why this waste? For this ointment
> could have been sold for a large sum, and the money given to the poor."
> —*Matthew 26:7-9*

It was 1993 and I was serving as the pastor of a struggling, declining, inner-city church that was in serious financial crisis. Since the 1970s its membership had dwindled from nearly a thousand to just a couple hundred, while the expense of maintaining ministry in its huge buildings had increased to a point *far* beyond the ability of its few members to support. Additionally, the age of the membership had grown dramatically to the point that, on Fathers Day, the *youngest* father present in worship was my sixty year old Dad. Therefore, not only were finances limited due to the size of the congregation, but the physical ability of the membership was limited due to their individual ages. It was an exceedingly difficult ministry setting with very few resources for doing ministry within the community. This failure was the real reason why this church was in such a serious predicament. While the congregation had remained predominately Anglo, the population around it had become heavily Hispanic. The

Church had stopped proclaiming the Gospel to the people who lived around it, and so it was dying.

Into this congregation I came and immediately was confronted with the harsh realities of being the pastor of a church that was suffering significant financial woes. One of the most difficult problems was the never-ending question of whether or not we would have enough money to simply pay our electric bill and meet our salaries … never mind having enough money to fund any kind of missional outreach! Financial life at this church was frequently hand-to-mouth, and so the occasional unexpected major gift was both greatly appreciated and greatly needed.

This was no truer than toward the end of my first year in the appointment, when many large bills were coming due. We were approximately ten thousand dollars in the hole and didn't know where we would get the money to make ends meet. On top of that, several of our most generous members were in the hospital, with at least one of them not expected to live much longer. It was a frightening month in the life of that church, and the stress on the staff was great. I'll never forget the day, mid-way through the last week of the year, when my secretary, Thelma, walked into my office and shakily handed me an opened envelope. I wasn't paying too much attention, so I didn't notice that she continued standing there, watching as I pulled out the letter and skimmed through the typed text. I then glanced at the attached check, grunted, and handed it back to her.

"You didn't see it, did you?" She asked.

"See what?"

She handed the letter back to me and I looked at the printed cashiers' check a second time. What I thought, at a glance, to be ten dollars turned out to be ten *thousand* dollars. It was precisely what the church needed to pay its year-end bills! It was, unquestionably, a miracle of God's grace. That unnamed person, through giving to the ministry of the church, had become an expression of God's love to us, an expression which exemplified the very heart of the sacramental nature of giving. Put simply, giving is a wonderful means of grace.

Unfortunately, rare is the individual who will think of giving as an instrument through which we receive the real presence of Jesus Christ. We are more accustomed to thinking of it as a duty or as an obligation—as a "good work"—not as a means of grace. However, when one examines the scriptural approach to giving it becomes quite clear that the act of giving is *far* more than an obligation. Indeed, the scriptures make it plain that, when we give of ourselves, of our personal, physical, and financial resources, God unleashes divine favor to us and, through us, to others. This is the fundamental essence of giving: in *every* respect it is a sacramental means of grace.

When we examine how giving functions in the religious life, we discover that no matter where it is found, it always has grace-filled characteristics. Specifically:

- When we give to God our emotional, physical, and financial gifts of praise, thanksgiving, and worship, God pours out to us the gifts of divine love and presence.
- When we receive God's grace through the gifts of others, we are called and empowered to join in giving to God.
- In this, our giving becomes a response to God's grace and a means of grace for us and for others.
- Jesus established that we are to give to others and, by giving to others, we give to him.

Giving is a means of grace. It is an instrument through which God opens to us the storehouse of divine love. It is a tool through which we receive the promises of Christ. When we act in faith and present our offerings to the Lord, God promises to shower us with favor.

While found in the Hebrew Bible, the following passage is nevertheless highly instructive to Christians who are approaching the means of grace from a sacramental perspective:

> Bring the full tithe into the storehouse, so that there
> may be food in my house, and thus put me to the test,

says the LORD of hosts; see if I will not open the windows of heaven for you and pour down for you an overflowing blessing.[189]

This is not some vague or undefined promise; it is a specific blessing tied to a specific act of giving. This is a very crucial point, and we should guard against super-spiritualizing it into non-existence. We are called to give. It's *not* any more difficult than that. We are called to open ourselves to the grace of God and give of the blessings that God has given us. This is not a spiritual metaphor, nor is it limited to just one kind of giving. We are called to make our offerings to God through the many ways that God has established. Some of these ways may appear to be unrelated to giving to God, but that is just an illusion of the human condition. In *all* of our Christian giving—and, especially, in the tithe—we are giving to the Lord.

Some Christians oppose the practice of tithing, claiming that since it was included in the Mosaic Covenant it has no place in Christian giving. They will rightly recognize that the role of the Law in determining our salvation ended with Christ.[190] From the Law we learn God's standard of righteousness, how far we fall short of that standard, and how much we are in need of God's grace. While keeping the Law does not save us, its role as our "school master" must not be undervalued.[191] In this respect, the tithe teaches us several important principles regarding giving. For instance, it serves as a guiding limitation on our giving. "How," you may ask? Keep in mind that Christian giving should be:

- "Cheerful" as an expression of the Holy Spirit.
- An indispensable component of faithful life.
- A Sacrificial expression of thanksgiving for all that we have received.

---

[189] Malachi 3:10
[190] Romans 10
[191] Galatians 3:24

- "Methodical," in that one's regular giving should be done according to a plan, or a schedule, or in a consistent way, and not haphazardly or lacking consistency.[192]

In considering these characteristics, it is clear that when a Christian is truly alive in the Spirit and motivated by God's grace to give, the tendency will be to give beyond any need that the Church might have. This was a serious issue in the First Century Church in Jerusalem and, based upon what can be gleaned from Paul's writings concerning the generosity of the Philippians, we can surmise that "over-giving" was a tendency elsewhere, as well. In response, the Biblical tithe can actually be understood as a limiting guideline, or brake, on the giving of Christians.

Far from being a demand for giving a minimum of 10%, tithing can rightly be understood—relative to the above characteristics—as setting a pattern for guidance to ensure that Christians do not give too much. Tithing helps to ensure that one's temporal needs are also met and proper provision is made for other financial responsibilities.

Critics of the tithe are correct in that, as a component of the Mosaic Covenant, its regulations are no longer in effect. We are made righteous by faith in Jesus Christ, not by keeping the law. Giving is an act of faith; and as such, it will be part of our faith-action which is accounted to us as righteousness. It's not a matter of "do this in order to be saved," but rather, "the saved, empowered by God's grace, deeply desire do this." In short, Christians are not only givers; when exercising their faith they are tithers.

Tithing pre-existed the Law. Just because it got adopted into the Law does not mean that tithing no longer has place as a means of grace. Just as faith pre-existed the law, being seated in Abraham's response to God's promise that he and Sarah would have children "like the stars of the heavens."[193] so also tithing is seated in Abraham's

---

[192]   See 2 Corinthians 8 & 9; 1 Corinthians 16:2; Galatians 6:6-10; Philippians 4:15-19; Mark 12:43; Acts 5

[193]   For an example, see Genesis 15:4–6

faith. Following Paul's reasoning, if the Covenant of Moses didn't abrogate the Covenant of Abraham—and it didn't[194]—it also didn't abrogate Abraham's faith-action of tithing as a response to God's grace and as a means of accessing further measures of that grace. We see this illustrated in Abraham's paying tithe to Melchizedek,[195] which pre-dated the Law and is referenced in direct relation to faith within the New Testament.

I believe that tithing is both an expression of the schoolmaster-function of the Law and, when exercised as faith-action, is a means of grace. As a component of the Law, it teaches us that we are not expected to give all of our money and resources; a set amount is sufficient. One may, of course, go beyond this set amount as offerings of thanksgiving, sweet savor, first fruits, and such; but the consistent pattern of giving is based on a set percentage as a reasonable portion of one's income. As an act of faith, it connects us to God's Grace; in conjunction with all the other means of grace, it furthers God's work of sanctification within us.

When we tithe we are returning to God that which is already Christ's. Jesus died for us—we are his possession—but God graciously gives back to us 90% of ourselves. How can we withhold the nominal 10% of not only our money, but also our prayers, presence, and service? Some might think that they can't afford to tithe, but in truth none of us can really afford to not tithe. The blessings of God's grace, which are promised to us when we act in faith, are just too precious to ignore.

The first and most obvious way of giving to God is by tithing to those ministries that have touched us, nurtured us, or through which we have found God's love meaningfully expressed. We are called to make our offering to God by giving to the church, and in so doing we give to those who have taught and nourished us in the Gospel. This shouldn't come as a surprise to any of us: giving to the community

---

[194]   Galatians 3:17
[195]   Genesis 14:20b; Hebrews 7:1–3

of faith has been taught to most cradle-to-grave Christians from their earliest childhood days. However, most probably haven't thought of this as a means of grace. And, yet, that is precisely what we find expressed in Paul's letter to his Church in Philippi:

> You Philippians indeed know that in the early days of the gospel, when I left Macedonia, no church shared with me in the matter of giving and receiving, except you alone. For even when I was in Thessalonica, you sent me help for my needs more than once. Not that I seek the gift, but I seek the profit that accumulates to your account. I have been paid in full and have more than enough; I am fully satisfied, now that I have received from Epaphroditus the gifts you sent, a fragrant offering, a sacrifice acceptable and pleasing to God. And my God will fully satisfy every need of yours according to his riches in glory in Christ Jesus.[196]

When the Philippians gave to Paul, their giving was a responsive act of faith that became a means of grace for the Apostle. This is what he was saying in his letter to the Philippians. Paul accepted their gift because he knew that their giving was an expression of their love of God and appreciation for God's ministry through the Apostle. Their giving was an outgrowth of God's grace within them, reaching out to Paul with thanksgiving for the gift of the Gospel they themselves had received. Paul had already been paid for his ministry, and was "fully satisfied," but he nevertheless received their gift as an expression of God's grace. He knew that it did the Philippians far *more* good to give than it did for him to receive. They gave because, through Paul's ministry, they had received the amazing

---

[196]   Philippians 4:15–19

Good News of salvation; Paul gave the Gospel in his ministry, and now he received the blessings of God's grace.

This is a perfect illustration of the cycle of grace in the Christian life. We receive the gift of grace, which we follow with our response of faith, and then our response of faith is followed by an even greater gift of grace, which occasions further responses of faith from us and even further gifts of grace from God ... and so forth. The Apostle tells the Philippians that the floodgates of God's love will be opened to them in response to their willingness to be open to God's love through giving. Indeed, Paul calls their cheerful gift to him a "fragrant offering" or an offering of "sweet savor" to God.[197] The image is of a liturgical offering of love and rejoicing, made out of sheer adoration for God and God's minister. When the Philippians gave to Paul, their gift was a "sweet savor" offering made to God *through* Paul.

The story from Matthew, with which we began this section, is a more direct expression of this kind of gift. Just as the Philippians were freely giving to Paul out of their love for the ministry of God in him, so also the woman who poured the alabaster jar of ointment over Jesus' head was freely giving to Christ out of her love for him. When we give to the church where we are nurtured in the faith, we are giving to Christ. This connection is rather easily made: the church is the Body of Christ, an image with which we should be familiar. We give to Christ Jesus by giving to the church our tithes and offerings; we give to God when we support those ministries and ministers who have supported us as under-shepherds of the Great Shepherd. When we give to our churches out of thanksgiving for the ministry we have received and the opportunities we have been given to proclaim our Savior to the entire world, we join with the woman in lavishing upon Christ our gifts of love. And, being a means of grace, when we give to Christ our giving accrues a direct benefit to us as well as to others.

---

[197]   For examples of sweet savor offerings, see especially Exodus 29:15–28 and Leviticus 2:1–11

Paul's words to his people in Corinth apply here as well. Referencing giving as an expression of the spirit in the Christian life, Paul wrote:

> The point is this: the one who sows sparingly will also reap sparingly, and the one who sows bountifully will also reap bountifully. Each of you must give as you have made up your mind, not reluctantly or under compulsion, for God loves a cheerful giver. And God is able to provide you with every blessing in abundance, so that by always having enough of everything, you may share abundantly in every good work.[198]

Yet again, it is important that we not attempt to spiritualize these words into meaninglessness; Paul is being very straightforward. When we give of our abundance simply because we desire to give— not out of guilt or because we feel it's a "must do"—God will pour into us even greater gifts of abundance. This should be understood in terms of literal, physical gifts, as well as spiritual gifts. When we give of our time, our talents, our gifts, and our service, God multiplies them for the benefit of the entire Body of Christ. We may hear snide remarks about how our gifts could have been better used elsewhere— to feed the hungry, clothe the naked, and provide for the poor—but we should be sure in the knowledge that God's grace will take and multiply our gifts to the glory of God's kingdom. God's kingdom includes the poor. In other words, when we give to God through the church, we can be assured that those in need will benefit as well.

This is the foundation for the sacramental character of the second form of giving. So many people want to try to separate giving to God from charitable giving to the poor and needy, as if both were not rooted in God's grace. But this is in *direct* contradiction to Jesus'

---

[198]   2 Corinthians 9:6-8

own identification of himself and his ministry with the poor. We are quick to want to spiritualize Jesus' words regarding the poor the same way the author of the Gospel of Matthew did: we, too, prefer to say "poor in spirit." While it is certainly true that the poor in spirit are promised blessings, Jesus affirms that when we give to the literal poor—to the sick, the hungry, the thirsty, those in prison—we are giving to *him*. This is nowhere more perfectly demonstrated than in Jesus' own words in a story from St. Matthew's Gospel:

> Then the king will say to those at his right hand, 'Come, you that are blessed by my Father, inherit the kingdom prepared for you from the foundation of the world; for I was hungry and you gave me food, I was thirsty and you gave me something to drink, I was a stranger and you welcomed me, I was naked and you gave me clothing, I was sick and you took care of me, I was in prison and you visited me.' Then the righteous will answer him, 'Lord, when was it that we saw you hungry and gave you food, or thirsty and gave you something to drink? And when was it that we saw you a stranger and welcomed you, or naked and gave you clothing? And when was it that we saw you sick or in prison and visited you?' And the king will answer them, 'Truly I tell you, just as you did it to one of the least of these who are members of my family, you did it to me.'[199]

When we give to the last, the least, and the lost in the name of Jesus, by faith we know we are giving *to* Jesus. And, when we give to Jesus through giving to others, the floodgates of God's grace are opened yet again to those to whom we give and to us as well. Our giving, however, doesn't originate with us. We give because we have been

---

[199]   Matthew 25:34-40

given to; we give because we have received. This is the *essence* of a sacramental means of grace: we first receive the love of God, then we respond by sharing this love with others, and then we receive again … and again and again … and the cycle of grace grows.

Our giving is not an obligation, nor is it a duty. Giving is a blessing, a calling, and a privilege. When we give we are honored to participate in a sacramental means of grace for others and, indeed, for ourselves. When we give of ourselves, of the many blessings we have received, we are sowing God's grace in our lives and in the lives of others. That which we sow we are promised that we will also reap, receiving the manifold blessings of God's grace in our lives and in the lives of the community of faith. As a sacramental means of grace, established by Christ and requiring our response of faith, giving is an *essential* component of the Christian life. It is an expression of our love for God and our faith in Jesus Christ as Lord and Savior. In all that we are and do, we are called to give.

Footwashing

> Then [Jesus] poured water into a basin and began to wash the disciples'
> feet and to wipe them with the towel that was tied around him.
> —*John 13:5*

Have you ever given much attention to your feet? I have mine. It's a sad thing that we cover them in socks and shoes and almost never bring them out for show. They're truly interesting, fascinating, awe-inspiring appendages. It may just be my opinion, but I think that God really produced an incredible work of art when feet came off the drawing board and went into production.

Next time you have a chance, take a close look at your feet. Hold your breath if you must, but give them a good looking over; you may be surprised at what you'll find. Did you know that each foot has a total of twenty-six bones? There are *seven* anklebones … imagine that! There are also *five* bones that make up your instep, which includes your heel bone. And as if this wasn't enough, you've also got a total of *fourteen* toe bones! That's a lot of bones! These are all held together and enabled to function by a vast array of interesting muscles and ligaments, principle of which is your *long plantar* ligament.[200] With all of these bones, ligaments, and muscles, it is no wonder our feet hurt so much after having been walked on all day long!

Feet become tired and achy, they become hot and sweaty, they become dirty and stinky. Even today, with regular baths and socks and shoes to keep out the dirt, our feet become somewhat less than attractive. And, so, we want to keep them hidden. Can you imagine, then, what it must have been like back during the days of Jesus, when most people didn't wear any kind of hosiery and frequently went around either barefoot or in sandals? Feet must have really hurt then. If we think our feet are ugly, dirty, and stinky today, just think about what your feet would have been like had you lived in a time when they went most of the day unprotected from the elements!

It is only logical that the practice of footwashing was both important for personal hygiene and popular for comfort; it is also logical that such a task was usually given over to the lowliest of servants. It certainly wasn't something that the master of a wealthy household would normally do; washing feet was menial labor that only those servants with no other skills were relegated to doing. And this is why it was such a great surprise to the disciples that Jesus would stoop to wash their feet.

John's Gospel tells us that on the night before Jesus was crucified he had a meal with his disciples. This meal is also described in the Synoptic Gospels, however in John instead of instituting the sacrament of Holy Communion, Jesus does something remarkably different. After the supper he:

---

[200]   John Clark, ed., *The Human Body: A Comprehensive Guide to the Structure and Functions of the Human Body* (New York: Arch Cape Press, 1989), 30.

...got up from the table, took off his outer robe, and
tied a towel around himself. Then he poured water
into a basin and began to wash the disciples' feet and
to wipe them with the towel that was tied around him.
He came to Simon Peter, who said to him, "Lord, are
you going to wash my feet?" Jesus answered, "You
do not know now what I am doing, but later you will
understand." Peter said to him, "You will never wash
my feet." Jesus answered, "Unless I wash you, you
have no share with me." Simon Peter said to him,
"Lord, not my feet only but also my hands and my
head!"[201]

We dare not be too hard on Peter, for we can easily understand his
reluctance to have Jesus wash his feet. Like Peter, we know that *we*
are the ones who should be serving our Lord; we should be washing
his feet, not the other way around. To have the King of kings and
the Lord of lords stooping down before us to perform a lowly act of
self-abasing service runs contrary to our expectations and our sense
of propriety. Deep down inside, in the very depths of our souls, we
know that we should be washing our *Lord's* feet; it is our place, our
duty, our proper role, to serve our Master. And yet, Jesus changed
this natural order when he knelt down to wash his disciples feet, took
the role of a slave, and reached out to cleanse us and make us whole.

Indeed, this is an image of the very incarnation itself, where
God becomes one of us in order to bridge the gap of sin that we have
created. Paul reflects on this fundamental theological proclamation
of the Christian faith when he recites the wonderful words of the
"Christ Hymn" in the course of his letter to the church in Philippi:

[Jesus] emptied himself, taking the form of a slave,
being born in human likeness. And being found in

---

[201]   John 13:4-9

human form, he humbled himself and became obedient
to the point of death—even death on a cross.[202]

Jesus became human not to be served but to serve; he was born to
be humbled and to die in our place. Rather than clinging to the glory
of his nature as God, the Second Person of the Holy Trinity emptied
himself into "the form of a slave," into the flesh-and-blood of our
human nature, a human nature that would then die for our sins. Just as
he was stripped and hung on the cross so that his death might cleanse
and make us whole, so here Jesus stripped himself and washed his
disciples' feet as both a symbol and an expression of the whole
gospel. Indeed, this simple act of service made evident the nature of
his presence and the life changing character of his death. In washing
his disciples feet, Jesus was performing a sacramental act which
makes understandable what it means for him to wash us clean of our
sins through his own self-giving on the cross. It is an encapsulated
representation of the doctrine of Substitutionary Atonement.

Washing feet was not something that one's master does; it was
an act of lowly service, of loving service, of self-giving service.
At its very core as an act of caring, it reflects the grace of God's
never-ending, unconditional love; its observance is surely a means
of grace with exceedingly strong sacramental characteristics. These
characteristics are no more clearly expressed than in what Jesus said
after he washed the disciples' feet:

> After he had washed their feet, had put on his robe,
> and had returned to the table, he said to them, "Do you
> know what I have done to you? You call me Teacher
> and Lord—and you are right, for that is what I am. So
> if I, your Lord and Teacher, have washed your feet,
> you also ought to wash one another's feet.[203]

---

[202]   Philippians 2:7–8
[203]   John 13:12–14

This commandment of the Lord is *very* similar to those that we have for celebrating the sacraments of Baptism and Holy Communion. In this passage we, like the disciples, are told that we are to "wash one another's feet." If we take this literally, as we take literally the directive to baptize and celebrate Communion, then we really should be washing each others' feet on a regular basis. The directive is not an option; Jesus didn't say: "if you want, you can wash one another's feet." Jesus' words were very clear. We are to wash one another's feet as an act of loving, self-giving service, and in so doing we will be expressing the love of God and the saving, cleansing grace of our savior Jesus Christ to each other.

The act of footwashing has all of the characteristics of a Christian sacrament:

- It is an act of faith.
- It is expressed through the common, everyday element of water, applied in humble service.
- Through this element of water the cleansing of our Lord's grace is symbolized.
- Through the means of service the grace of Jesus is offered to those who respond in faith.
- The recipient is passive, receiving the action, and then is invited to actively respond by doing the same for others.
- Jesus instituted the act with his disciples.

Each point is important. We are called to act in faith in the washing of each other's feet. We are to use simple water, and to perform this act of service humbly kneeling before our brothers and sisters in Christ. In so doing, we express the self-giving love and grace of God in terms that reflect the incarnation, death, and resurrection of our Savior. And, we are called to do this because Jesus told us to do so.

Yet it is not merely a good work, or an ordinance that we do just because Jesus ordered us to. It is a means of grace for the person who does the washing as well as a means of grace for the one who receives it. It is a means of grace when we wash, for in our washing of our fellow disciples' feet we learn what it means for us to serve as Jesus served, to give of ourselves in order to provide cleansing for our sisters and brothers in Christ. When we wash another's feet, we experience just a little bit of the self-giving love that Jesus had in great abundance for everyone; it is this love that we are called to express to others by washing their feet.

It is also a means of grace when we receive the washing; for through it we experience anew the humbling reality that Jesus, who didn't have to kneel and serve, who didn't have to give himself to cleanse us of our sins, nevertheless did. He gave himself up in our place, as an eternal act of self-giving service, so that we might be washed clean and made whole. When our brother or sister kneels before us in humble service, washing our stinky feet, we experience the grace of discovery, the grace of realization, that God loves us despite our stinky feet. Jesus expresses this love to us, even though we do not deserve it; and so we are called to express this love to others.

A Sacrament or a Sacramental?

Footwashing, like forgiveness, healing, marriage, ordination, prayer, and even giving, has all of the characteristics of a sacrament, but isn't one. It is a means of grace which was established by Christ Jesus and to which we have the duty to respond. Like the others, it is sacramental in nature, but is not--for most Protestants—a sacrament.

In my opinion this distinction is, in most of these cases, quite artificial. Take footwashing: it has the ability to connect us directly to the real presence of Jesus in our fellow believers when they kneel to wash our feet. It takes eyes of faith to see our Lord, kneeling at our feet to perform a lowly act of service. It takes faith; but if we truly open ourselves to God's grace we can and will see Jesus in our dear sister or brother—just as, with eyes of faith, we can discern the real presence of Jesus in the bread and in the wine of the Eucharist. And, so, I have serious problems in making a clear distinction between the sacramentals, like footwashing or forgiveness, and the two sacraments. And, yet, my Protestant sensibilities can understand the reasons why the sacraments have been limited to just the principle two. Throughout its history, the Church has been nearly unanimous in identifying Communion and Baptism as being the most blessed means of grace.

The other sacramentals have had varying degrees of affirmation by Christians; and while they have also been almost unanimously considered means of grace, their nature as being sacraments has been open for interpretation. In the final equation, I must agree that there is a qualitative difference, albeit a *small* one, between these sacramentals and the two principle sacraments. They are all means, they are all instruments which aid us in receiving God's wonderful, life-transforming grace. However, they are not all the same, or of equal importance, in communicating the real presence of Jesus Christ to us. As important as forgiveness, healing, marriage, ordination, prayer, giving, and footwashing are as means of grace for the Christian community's faith-expression, they are secondary as methods through which we receive the love and favor of our Savior.

Questions for Reflection and Discussion

Chapter Six

♦ According to its definition in this chapter, what is a sacramental?

♦ In addition to those listed in this book, can you think of other sacramentals?

♦ Have you ever made a confession of sin with the assistance of a minister? If so, describe the feeling before, during, and after the experience.

♦ If you haven't, are there any reasons why you haven't? If you would like to, do you believe your pastor would be willing to help you in this? If not, why not?

♦ What does it mean to be healed? Is there a difference between healing and curing?

♦ If you are married, describe what is important for you in maintaining your marriage.

♦ If you are not married, reflect upon God's presence in your life and consider the ways in which, in your singleness, you may live a life married to God.

♦ What is the meaning of ordination?

♦ Do you believe that there is any difference between lay people and ordained ministers?

◆ Do you have a discipline of prayer, or do you just pray when you feel the need?

◆ What role does giving play in your Christian life?

◆ Do you tithe (give 10% of your income) to your Church? Do you give beyond a simple tithe? Do you give to the needy through your Church, or do you reach out beyond the ministries of your Church?

◆ Have you ever participated in a footwashing service? What did it feel like to have someone else wash your feet?

◆ How does footwashing reflect the ministry of Jesus?

I Love the Word of God

I love the Word of God,
It is so dear to me.
It is God's Love revealed to us,
And given, O so free!

I love the Word of God,
It gives so much to me.
It makes God's Holy Presence real,
Enables us to see.

I love the Word of God,
The power divine in me.
God's grace will make us ready now,
God's Glory to receive.

I love the Word of God,
Written upon my heart.
God's Joy established in my soul,
A Holy, spiritual art.

I love the Word of God,
It clears my blinded eyes.
Enables me to humbly love,
And praises now shall rise!

Gregory S. Neal †
June, 1998

Chapter Seven

The Scriptures as Means of Grace

When we speak of the Scriptures as being a means of grace, what do we mean? Baptism, Holy Communion, forgiveness, healing, marriage, ordination, prayer, giving, footwashing—all of these means of grace should make sense to us; we can see how they function in our lives to communicate to us the love and real presence of Jesus. Their character as sacraments and sacramental acts should be abundantly clear to us. Can the same be said for the Holy Scriptures? How do they function as means of grace?

I submit that the Scriptures function in an indispensable and fundamental way as a means of grace for us: they communicate the real presence of Jesus Christ—the Incarnate Word of God—through the words, thoughts, ideas, and experiences of the Biblical authors. In this way, they provide us with a link to the living experience of the risen Christ in the early Church and to the transforming reality of that experience, which still has power to justify and sanctify us today.

One excellent statement on the nature of the Scriptures can be found in the Anglican and Methodist Articles of Religion:

> The Holy Scriptures containeth all things necessary
> to salvation; so that whatsoever is not read therein, nor
> may be proved thereby, is not to be required of any

man that it should be believed as an article of faith,
or be thought requisite or necessary to salvation.[204]

This doctrinal position, coming from a major Protestant tradition, should make it clear that the Bible is central to Christian life and faith. The Bible is authoritative because it is the norm by which the requirements for salvation are established. If a theological opinion or belief is not found in the scriptures, or if it otherwise cannot be supported through a careful study of the Scriptures, then it *cannot* be required that a person believe it. The bible establishes the outer boundaries for belief; it also outlines the inner boundaries for our Christian living. After all, the Scriptures are described as "containing all things necessary to salvation." This is a powerful proclamation and goes directly to the core of their identity as an important means of grace. The Scriptures are a means of grace specifically in that they "contain all things necessary to salvation." What else is grace if it isn't God's saving love manifested in the lives of believers? As a means of grace, the Scriptures bring salvation to those who receive them.

But there remains the important question: how do they do this? How does a simple book, a collection of thoughts, words, and ideas, become a means of grace for us? How do they contain God's grace, and how does this grace get to us? I believe that they convey God's grace because they reconnect us to the resurrection experience of the early church, which wrote them.

---

[204]   Article V, The Methodist Articles of Religion, *The Book of Discipline of The United Methodist Church, 2012.*

Authority and Inspiration as Means of Grace

The sum of your word is truth; and every one of your
righteous ordinances endures forever.
—*Psalm 119:160*

In what are we to ground the authority of the Holy Scriptures? Do we assume a literal inerrancy of each word of the Bible? Do we turn to a few selected teachings of Jesus, which make up a "Canon within a Canon?" Or, do we turn to the living community of the faith as providing authority for the Bible? If the church of Jesus Christ is going to be faithful to its heritage, as well as to its current situation, it is first going to have to make a decision as to how to ground its own authority. Each of the three suggested locations have something of an appeal to them, but in their entirety *each* fails to provide an adequate answer to the question of Biblical authority.

On the surface, the first one makes life easy. The Bible is to be accepted as the "Inerrant Word of God," leaving no room for ambiguity, no need for questions, and no place for debate or alternative interpretation. Everything one needs to know in order to live a Christian life is written in the pages of the Bible. The Bible is the first and last arbiter, the sole source for ethical discourse, and the *final* authority on all subjects from morality, philosophy, and history, to physics, biology, and cosmology. The Bible is understood as being *literally* true, both in spirit and, most especially, in word. Indeed, each and every word is viewed as being *necessarily* without error because God has verbally dictated it to the Biblical authors.

As comforting as such an approach might be to many, the simple fact is that biblical inerrancy ignores the greater body of evidence demonstrating that the Bible is *not* literally inerrant, nor was it verbally dictated by God. A detailed study of the Bible demonstrates that it is a dynamic collection of diverse literature written by many different people over several thousand years of time, all living in communion with each other as well as with God.

The second possibility is attractive because it requires us to consider Jesus' teachings as being normative for the Christian community. This is usually accomplished through an in-depth "search for the historical Jesus," in which the biblical account is sifted to determine the actual particulars of the historical Rabbi from Nazareth. The results of this process are then systematized to aid in constructing an ethic for Christian living. The advantage of this approach is that it requires the church to take seriously what the Scriptures say. Even where the Biblical witness is largely set aside, at least the early church's faith in Christ has been considered. The problem with this is that what is thereby determined to be "authentic" is usually promoted as being *all* that is needed. The early church's interpretation of the sayings of Jesus is almost *totally* disregarded in favor of what amounts to an artificially "reconstructed Jesus," one who usually looks rather more like an idealized religious guru of twentieth and twenty-first century counter-culture than a first century Jewish Rabbi. The "biblical Jesus" is generally ignored as religious authority becomes increasingly seated in the modern critical community's rational ability to determine what is truly from "the historical Jesus," and what is just "theological accretion."

The third possibility is appealing because it provides much latitude for belief and practice. Individual experience becomes the final arbiter of the Christian stance on any issue. Reference to the Bible and the tradition of the Church may be made, but if it conflicts with the experiential truth of the living community, one or both must be set aside in favor of the more relevant witness of life. This is, of course, faulty from its inception: who is to say that the current community's needs, thoughts, and goals are more appropriate than those of the community which first experienced Christ?

The question of authority is not an easy one, nor should the location of authority be understood as definable within neat boundaries. Quite the contrary; what I propose is that a dynamic interrelationship between the original community of the faithful and the living community of the faithful be established which would allow for both authority and its interpretation to be carried out within the locus of the Holy Scriptures.

The early church remembered Jesus. During the time of the Apostle Paul, there were many Christians who could remember both the pre-crucifixion Jesus and the risen Lord; and this situation lingered for many decades. This experience of the church—an experience of God, breaking into time—was what formed the church. Indeed, this experience of God in Christ resulted in such a powerful and enduring change in the lives of the early Christians that its memory could not be wiped away by time or oppression. It continued to resonate in their preaching and teaching, living and dying, to the second and third generations and, eventually, on to today. But by the end of the second generation most of what is now within the New Testament had been written. In these writings we find a mixture of the oral traditions, theological reflections, and historical situations of the early church. This is the record of those who either knew Jesus during his life here on earth or were in close contact with those who did. This is their account of the event which created the church *and* their reaction to that event. As such, the Scriptures are the creation of the community as well as of the holy event itself. And it is this situation, this event, this community, and their experience of the resurrection, which is the basis for the grace that the Scriptures communicate to us today.

This grace comes in many ways: through a simple reading, through serious study, through preaching, through song and dance, the Scriptures come alive with a transforming power for us in ways that go beyond our ability to catalog. And indeed, isn't that always true concerning God's marvelous grace? When it comes to God's grace, we are always merely scratching the surface of the immeasurable depths of God's love.

While the scriptures contain the Word of God, they also contain the words of human beings. God inspired the Bible, true; but God did so through the instrumentality of human beings, with human words and human thoughts and human experiences playing a large role in the writing. The human authors, through whom God worked in the writing of the Scriptures, were still human beings as they wrote: they had human failings, human opinions, human agendas, human dreams and desires. They didn't stop being human, nor did they give up their identity, their ingenuity, or their personal characteristics as they wrote.

We are sometimes tempted by those in the conservative wing of the Church to view the process of inspiration as a suspension of the human will and identity in order to take some kind of "divine dictation." However, any balanced, open-eyed, reasonable approach to the Biblical record will reveal that such a complete take-over of human identity simply didn't happen. Each of the canonical books shows clear and unmistakable signs of its human author: the author's character, humor, political and historical opinions, biases and bigotries, all come through in each and every book of the Bible.

Christians are correct in affirming that God had an important and unmistakable role in the writing of the Bible, and we should never go so far as to deny the presence of divine inspiration within our Scriptures. However, as we do this, we do the Scriptures a grave injustice if we fail to recognize that the Bible is still a collection of human reflections and opinions upon our encounter with God. As a people of faith, we should be ready to recognize that both characteristics are true; and we should seek ways of interpreting the Bible which take into account the dynamic interplay between the divine Word and human thought.

This brings up the important question: what do we mean by "inspiration"? If we don't mean a suspension of human will and identity, then what *do* we mean? Perhaps one of the best ways of illustrating what many Christians mean by "inspiration" is to take a look at some of the other ways in which we use the word. For example, we often say that a sunrise, sunset, or other sight of great beauty will "inspire" us to write a wonderful poem or paint a remarkable painting or compose a powerful song. The sight so "moves" us, so "compels" us, so "empowers" us, so "inspires" us, that we put our emotional and intellectual response into creative action; we produce a work of art that contains within it a degree of the beauty and emotion that originally "inspired" us.

That is certainly a kind of inspiration, and it is one of the ways in which we may indeed view the inspiration of the Bible. God so moved in the lives of the Biblical authors that their response to God's presence and action was to write their reflections upon these events and upon what they believed God was trying to say to and through them. While I don't believe that this is the only kind of inspiration to be found in the Bible, I do believe that it is a major form that is often overlooked.

I ask you: do we normally reproduce that which inspires us with precision and stark reality? No, we present our interpretation of that which inspires us. When we want to exactly reproduce that which inspires us, all we have to do is take a photograph or make an audio recording! With a great deal of artistic production, however, the idea is to present that which inspires us with the human interpretation serving as an important component in the communication. This is, I believe, far closer to what we mean by "the Inspiration of the Holy Scriptures" than are concepts of dictation. Yes, I *do* believe that we have communications from God in the Holy Scriptures. I believe in Divine Revelation. However, I also believe that much of that communication comes to us through human interpretations, with human words and human grammar and human biases and human agendas, all sometimes sharing equal billing with what God is saying.

How does this kind of divine inspiration actually function in the context of the writing of the Holy Scriptures? Let's take the Gospels, and specifically the Gospel of Luke, as our example. The author of this particular Gospel *nowhere* asserts that he was physically present at the events he describes. What he is writing is the product of his research, his scholarship, his painstaking interviews of those who were present at the events, and/or of those who heard the stories of those who were present at the events. Luke wrote not as an eyewitness, but rather as a theologian and historian. Luke took the written works of those who came before him, particularly the Gospel of Mark and a collection of Jesus' sayings which was also available to the author of the Gospel of Matthew; he crafted his Gospel in such a way as to present the story of the birth, life, ministry, death, and resurrection of Jesus. This presentation contains Luke's theological interpretation of the events, along with the theological interpretations of the community of faith in which he lived and of the disciples and apostles who went before him. All of this is fairly certain, based upon what we see in Luke's Gospel as well as in Mark and Matthew.[205]

The inspiration of the Holy Spirit comes into play in the writing of the Bible as the clear compelling motivation that drove the authors to write. Luke set out to write his Gospel because the Holy Spirit compelled him to write; the memories and experiences of those whom he interviewed were empowered by the inspiration of the Holy Spirit. This same inspiration is also present in the theological interpretation of the early Church, as well as in their creative poetry and vision. There are many avenues for inspiration to function without our having to twist the clear character of the Bible in order to assert that God dictated each and every word to the authors. God inspired them and the sources they used, and so they wrote; and what they wrote included both inspired material *and* material that comes from the perspective and the biases and even the faulty memories of the authors and their sources. And even through all of this, the word of God still comes through with the power to save us.

This presence of the Holy Spirit makes the Holy Scriptures a means of grace.

---

[205] For the authorship of the Synoptic Gospels (Matthew, Mark, and Luke), see any current textbook on the formation of the New Testament. For example: Raymond E Brown, *An Introduction to the New Testament* (New Haven: Yale University Press, 1997).

Questions for Reflection and Discussion

Chapter Seven

♦ What does the Bible mean to you, and what role does it play in your Christian life?

♦ How does the Bible serve as a means of grace?

♦ How frequently do you read your Bible?

♦ Is there a difference between "The Word of God" and the Bible?

♦ What do you believe it means to say that the Bible is "inspired?"

♦ Have you ever felt inspired by God?

Upon The Cross

Upon that Old Rugged Cross He hung
    In the hot sunshine,
Convicted of every crime and sin
    Committed since Adam's time.

God came down to Earth for this
    God gave His Son to die,
God's love was revealed Upon The Cross
    And in the blood, pooling at its side.

Oh, to put your finger in the blood
    And gaze upon the lamb,
And know that all the mighty power of God
    Was visible, that day, in all the land.

And in that moment, when God cried
    And when Our Lord did die,
The sunshine ceased, the Earth was shook
    and Heaven's gates did open wide.

Oh, to be present on that day,
    To stand, to kneel, to cry and watch,
As all the mysteries of God's Grace
    Came to light upon His face.

Gregory S. Neal†
November 1993

204

Chapter Eight

Skipping Stones and the Means of Grace

Have you ever been skipping stones on a river and noticed that the object is not always to get the thinnest, most perfect rock that you can find? Sometimes it's better to throw one of the thicker, less-rounded stones. Sometimes the irregular stones are better. Sometimes the heavier stones go farther. And the same is true with life.

The trick to skipping stones is not all in the choice of rock. A great deal depends upon how you throw the stone, the lateral "spin" you give it, and its angle when it hits the water. After many tries, proper wrist action can make up for almost any irregularity in the shape of your rock. And the number of skips on the surface is often directly proportional to the velocity and angle of the rock against the surface of the water—but not always.

I can remember choosing a very thin, almost perfectly rounded stone; I brushed off the dirt and mud that clung to it and then I flung it out towards the water. I did everything right: I had cocked my wrist to give the stone a spin; I had angled the stone so that it would impact the surface of the water at about a ten degree angle in the direction of its motion; and I had given it more than enough velocity. It should have navigated five or six skips, easily.

It sank after only two hops! I was so disappointed.

Next, in frustrated anger, I chose a larger rock, thick at its midpoint, irregular in its shape, and at least three or four times heavier than the first rock. It had the aerodynamics of a Methodist

Hymnal—which is to say, none at all. I cocked my arm with just about all of my strength, intending to release that stone with a vicious spin. Unfortunately, I felt the rock slip in my fingers as I threw it, and its spin was off center just enough to make it wobble with vicious irregularity. Certainly it would plop under the water upon initial impact … right?

It skipped six times!

Sometimes life is definitely like that. You can be doing everything right, you can be careful in your planning, in your preparations, and in your dedication to what you believe is true. You can put all of your energy and resources into your endeavors, you can struggle to make everything perfect, but things still fizzle. You only get two lousy skips out of your best, most carefully executed efforts.

Other times you apparently do everything wrong, are sloppy in your planning and inattentive in your course of action; and yet, somehow, everything turns out all right! Despite everything, you get six skips!

Why? Why do our best-laid plans fail, but when we give up trying to be in control God steps in to work a miracle? Why is God's grace so much more effective than our most capable attempts?[206]

I submit that it has *everything* to do with our unwillingness to let go of our own desires, our own dreams, and our own expectations of what will make us happy. We think we know what is best. We think we know the source of true joy, when in truth we are only fooling ourselves. We thrash around throughout our lives and never find joy because we're always looking in the wrong places. We treat life like a fishing tournament, believing "the one who catches the most fish wins," never realizing that we've missed the whole point.

The Mountain Fork River, in southeast Oklahoma, is one of the most beautiful rivers I have ever seen. When fishing along Beaver's Bend, just below the old dam, the water is so clear that it's actually

---

[206]   1 Corinthians 1:25 – "For God's foolishness is wiser than human wisdom, and God's weakness is stronger than human strength."

possible to see the fish maneuvering under the water to go after your bait. The unfortunate thing about this is that if you can see the fish, the fish can see you. And so, it's best to fish further out toward the middle—far enough away so that the little buggers can't see you. It's not obvious at first, but with practice I have discovered that it's the best, most enjoyable way to catch dinner.

But be careful! To get your cast to go that far you've got to put a lot of energy into it, and that can throw you off your balance and cause more problems than it's worth. Furthermore, the rocks you're standing on are very slippery and the trees behind you on the riverbank like to catch your line when you're on your backward cast. This makes for some frustrated thrashing and some colorful, unchristian-like language; both of which are guaranteed to scare away the fish and make you look silly. Nothing is worse than becoming frustrated when fishing. I go fishing for the fun of it, not to "bag my limit." And yet, I'm frequently frustrating myself.

Sometimes the truth is staring us right in the face, but we're too blind to see it. That's the way things are with the deep, spiritual truths of life. We can try to shroud them in intelligent-sounding, highly educated, polysyllabic terms, but that is just window dressing. The deep truths of life still evade our understanding. We may experience them, but we can never fully *understand* them.

Just as the really deep truths of this life are not always obvious, so also the joy and the really great successes of our lives are rarely our own doing. Apart from God's love, mercy, and grace, we get our metaphorical lines caught in the metaphorical trees, or we slip off of the metaphorical rocks and into the metaphorical—but still quite cold and swift—currents of life. We may think we're good at fishing; in reality, we're just going through the motions and causing more problems than we solve. Sometimes it's not worth it to try and catch that little goggle-eye; on the other hand, just watching him play with your bait while he watches you play with him *is* worth it!

Sometimes a perceived disadvantage can be an incredible advantage. This is nowhere more true than when it comes to our utter helplessness in things that are spiritual. The problem is that we are so reticent to recognize that we really *are* helpless. It's when we fool ourselves into thinking that we can achieve God's will on our own that we royally mess things up. Just look at Abram and Hagar, producing Ishmael in an attempt to accomplish God's will *for* God! That's an excellent example of the kind of trouble that our human arrogance in spiritual matters can produce.[207] And, yet, we do this kind of thing all the time. We thrash around, swing our rod and line, cast back and get caught in the trees, slip off the rocks of life, and end up all wet in our attempts to do for *ourselves* what God has promised to do for us! In the terms of this metaphor, we get so focused on the fishing that we lose sight of the simple joy of just living.

Sometimes the size of the rock is not important. Sometimes the angle and speed of release is not important. Sometimes the bigger, irregular rocks work better. And quite often, we learn a lot more from our own failures than we do from our success. We can throw all our effort into skipping stones, and they might or might not skip at all. We can cast far away and catch that fish, but we might not have nearly as much fun as we would have just watching as the fish watches us. We can try and try and try, but if we ignore the grace of God, and the love and joy that God has for us, we will surely *fail*.

We try to do things, we try to accomplish God's will, we try to pray, we try to act, we try to serve, and we end up with a *we*-ism … a religion that focuses on the self and not upon God. One of the beautiful things about the sacramental approach to grace is that its focus is God, never us. Baptism, Communion, forgiveness, healing, prayer, giving, confirmation—Christians do not *do* any of these things. It might look as if we do them, but that is a misinterpretation of spiritual reality. These means of grace are the outward manifestations of God's wonderful work of love in our lives. In the Christian life God is *always* the primary actor. We initiate nothing; we simply respond.

---

[207]   Genesis 16; see, also, Paul's interpretation of this story found in Galatians 4:21-31. Note, this really isn't a commentary on Ishmael or Hagar; rather, its focus is upon Abram's attempt to accomplish God's will in a way that made sense to him rather than in the way that God ordained.

I am convinced that we never succeed by our actions alone. What success we do have in living the Christian life comes to us solely through the grace of God. All we can do is respond, while finding our joy in the beauty of God's grace. Sometimes it's just fun to watch as God works through our imperfections to make miracles happen.

The joy of living is the whole point of fishing and of skipping stones. It's also the wondrous reality of the means of grace. We're called to find joy in this life; but until we look to God, any joy that we may find is an illusion. Through the means of grace, through the sacraments and the sacramentals, God provides us with what we need—the love, joy, and real presence of Jesus Christ—to proclaim the Gospel in word and in deed. Our lives as Christians are empowered entirely by the love of God, so much so that, apart from God's love, we can do nothing. That is why the means of grace are so important. We are called to receive grace upon grace from the very fullness of God in Jesus Christ our Lord. It is this grace that empowers us, improves us, and moves us. It is by this grace that we live.

Questions for Reflection and Discussion

Chapter Eight

♦ What is the role of the means of grace in your life?

♦ Having read this book, and having thought about the means of grace, do you discern a place in your life where God's grace is missing? If so, describe it.

♦ How might the means of grace help you in living a faithful Christian life?

Selected Bibliography

T he works included in this Bibliography cover a wide range of theological and Biblical thought. Included are the works cited in the footnotes of this book, as well as a number of the works that have made a substantial contribution to the author's thinking on systematic theology in general and sacramental theology in particular. Many of the works are out of print and some are exceedingly rare. I would like to offer my thanks to the Interlibrary Loan Office of Fondren Library and to the Reference staff at Bridwell Library, both at Southern Methodist University, for their help in obtaining several of the more hard-to-get books.

***

Allison, C. FitzSimons. *The Cruelty of Heresy: An Affirmation of Christian Orthodoxy.* Harrisburg: Morehouse Publishing, 1994.

Arminius, James. *The Works of James Arminius.* Grand Rapids: Baker Book House, 1986.

Baptism, Eucharist, and Ministry. Geneva: The World Council of Churches, 1982.

Bauer, Walter, ed. *A Greek-English Lexicon of the New Testament and Other Early Christian Literature.* Chicago: University of Chicago Press, 1979.

Beasley-Murray, G.R. *Baptism: In The New Testament.* Grand Rapids: William B. Eerdman's Publishing Co., Inc., 1962.

Benson, Richard Meux. *Look To The Glory.* Reprint. Cambridge: Cowley Press, 1965.

The Book of Common Prayer and Administration of the Sacraments and other Rites and Ceremonies of the Church According to the use of The Episcopal Church. Boston: Seabury Press, 1979.

The Book of Discipline of The United Methodist Church. Nashville: The United Methodist Publishing House, 2012.

The Book of Worship of The United Methodist Church. Nashville: The United Methodist Publishing House, 1992.

Borgen, Ole E. *John Wesley on the Sacraments.* Grand Rapids: Francis Asbury Press, 1985.

Bouyer, Louis. *Eucharist: Theology and Spirituality of the Eucharistic Prayer.* Notre Dame: University of Notre Dame, 1968.

Bromiley, Geoffrey. *Historical Theology: An Introduction.* Edinburgh: T&T Clark, 1978.

Brown, Harold O. J. *Heresies.* Garden City: Doubleday, 1984.

Brown, Raymond E. *An Introduction to the New Testament.* New Haven: Yale University Press, 1997.

Campbell, Dennis M. *The Yoke of Obedience: The Meaning of Ordination in Methodism.* Nashville: Abingdon Press, 1989.

The Catechism of the Catholic Church. Liguori: Libreria Editrice Vaticana, 1994.

Clark, Francis. *Eucharistic Sacrifice and the Reformation.* Devon: Augustine Publishing Company, 1967.

Clark, John, ed. *The Human Body: A Comprehensive Guide to the Structure and Functions of the Human Body.* New York: Arch Cape Press, 1989.

Collins, Kenneth J. *The Scripture Way of Salvation: The Heart of John Wesley's Theology.* Nashville: Abingdon Press, 1997.

Collins, Kenneth J. *The Theology of John Wesley: Holy Love and the Shape of Grace.* Nashville: Abingdon Press, 2007.

Collins, Kenneth J. *Wesley on Salvation: A Study in the Standard Sermons.* Grand Rapids: Francis Asbury Press, 1989.

Conzelmann, Hans. *1 Corinthians.* Philadelphia: Fortress Press, 1975.

Cullmann, Oscar. *Baptism In The New Testament.* Philadelphia: The Westminster Press, 1950.

Cullmann, Oscar, F.J. Leenhardt. *Essays On The Lord's Supper.* Richmond: John Knox Press, 1958.

Dale, James W. *Christic Baptism and Patristic Baptism.* Wauconda: Bolchazy-Carducci Publishers, 1874/1994.

Donlan, Thomas C., Francis L.B. Cunningham, and Augustine Rock. *Christ, And His Sacraments.* Dubuque: The Priory Press, 1958.

Felton, Gayle Carlton. *This Holy Mystery: A United Methodist Understanding of Holy Communion.* Nashville: Discipleship Resources, 2005.

Felton, Gayle C. *United Methodists and the Sacraments.* Nashville: Abingdon Press, 2007.

Fiorenza, Francis Schussler and John P. Galvin, eds. *Systematic Theology: Roman Catholic Perspectives.* 2 Vols. Minneapolis: Fortress Press, 1991.

Gerrish, B. A. *Grace and Gratitude: The Eucharistic Theology of John Calvin.* Minneapolis: Fortress Press, 1993.

Groeschel, Benedict J. and James Monti. *In The Presence of Our Lord: The History, Theology, and Psychology of Eucharistic Devotion.* Steubenville: Franciscan University Press, 1996.

Gutwenger, Englebert. *Encyclopedia of Theology.* New York: Crossroad Publishing Co., 1976.

Hardon, John A. *With Us Today: On the Real Presence of Jesus Christ in the Eucharist.* Naples: Sapientia Press, 2000.

Heitzenrater, Richard P. *The Illusive Mr. Wesley*: *2 Vols.* Nashville: Abingdon Press, 1987.

Heitzenrater, Richard P. *Wesley and the People called Methodists.* Nashville: Abingdon Press, 1994.

Hodge, Charles. *Systematic Theology: 3 Vols.* Grand Rapids: Wm. B. Eerdmans Publishing Co., 1989.

Hunsinger, George. *The Eucharist and Ecumenism: Let us Keep the Feast.* Cambridge: Cambridge University Press, 2008.

Irwin, Kevil W. *Models of the Eucharist.* New York: Paulist Press, 2005.

Israel, Martin. *Healing as Sacrament.* Cambridge: Cowley Publications, 1984.

Jackson, Thomas, ed. *The Works of John Wesley, 3rd Edition,* Reprint. Grand Rapids: Baker Books, 1972.

Jeremias, Joachim. *The Eucharistic Words of Jesus.* London: SCM Press, Ltd., 1987.

Kelly, J.N.D. *Early Christian Doctrines.* London: Adam & Charles Black, 1968.

Kinghorn, Kenneth Cain. *The Gospel of Grace: The Way of Salvation in the Wesleyan Tradition.* Nashville: Abingdon Press, 1992.

Khoo, Lorna Lock-Nah. *Wesleyan Eucharistic Spirituality: Its Nature, Sources and Future.* Adelaide: ATF Press, 2005.

Klaiber, Walter *Living Grace: An Outline of United Methodist Theology.* Nashville: Abingdon Press, 2001.

Lang, Jovian, ed. *Dictionary of the Liturgy.* New York: Catholic Book Publishing Co., 1989.

Langford, Thomas. *Practical Divinity: Theology in the Wesleyan Tradition.* Nashville: Abingdon Press, 1983.

LaVerdiere, Eugene. *The Eucharist in the New Testament and the Early Church.* Collegeville: The Liturgical Press, 1996.

Maddox, Randy L. *Responsible Grace: John Wesley's Practical Theology.* Nashville: Kingswood Books, 1994.

Micks, Marianne. *Deep Waters: An Introduction to Baptism.* Cambridge: Cowley Publications, 1999.

Mitchell, Nathan. *Real Presence: The Work of Eucharist.* Chicago: Liturgical Training Publications, 1998.

Morrill, Bruce T. *Encountering Christ in the Eucharist: The Paschal Mystery in People, Word, and Sacrament.* New York: Paulist Press, 2012.

Norwood, Frederick. *The Story of American Methodism.* Nashville: Abingdon Press, 1974.

O'Connor, James T. *The Hidden Manna: A Theology of the Eucharist.* San Francisco: Ignatius Press, 1988.

Oden, Thomas C. *The Transforming Power of Grace.* Nashville: Abingdon Press, 1993.

O'Neill, Colman E. *Meeting Christ in the Sacraments.* New York: Alba House, 1991.

Pohle, Joseph. *The Sacraments: A Dogmatic Treatise.* Vol. 1, *The Sacraments in General. Baptism, Confirmation.* London: B. Herder Book Co., 1946.

Ramsey, Michael. *The Gospel and the Catholic Church.* Reprint. Cambridge: Cowley Press, 1990.

Rattenbury, J. Ernest. *The Eucharistic Hymns of John and Charles Wesley.* Cleveland: OSL Publications, 1990.

Ratzinger, Joseph Cardinal. *God Is Near Us: The Eucharist, the Heart of Life.* San Francisco: Ignatius Press, 2003.

Richter, Klemens. *The Meaning of the Sacramental Symbols: Answers to Today's Questions.* Collegeville: The Liturgical Press, 1990.

Roberts, Alexander and James Donaldson, eds. *Ante-Nicene Fathers.* 10 Vols. Peabody MA: Hendrickson Publishers, Inc., 1995.

Robertson, Archibald and Alfred Plummer. *A Critical and Exegetical Commentary On The First Epistle of St. Paul to the Corinthians.* Edinburgh: T&T Clark, Limited, 1986 [Reprint].

Schaff, Philip, ed. *Nicene and Post-Nicene Fathers, First and Second Series.* 28 Vols. Peabody MA: Hendrickson Publishers, Inc., 1995.

Schmemann, Alexander. *The Eucharist.* Crestwood: St. Vladimir's Press, 1988.

Schmemann, Alexander *For The Life Of The World: Sacraments and Orthodoxy.* Crestwood: St. Vladimir's Press, 1988.

Shillebeeckx, Edward *Christ: The Experience of Jesus as Lord.* New York: Crossroad Press, 1980.

Smith, Martin ed., *Benson of Cowley.* Cambridge: Cowley Publications, 1983.

Stamm, Mark W. *Sacraments & Discipleship: Understanding Baptism and the Lord's Supper in a United Methodist Context.* Nashville: Discipleship Resources, 2001.

Staples, Rob L. *Outward Sign and Inward Grace: The Place of the Sacraments in Wesleyan Spirituality.* Kansas City: Beacon Hill Press of Kansas City, 1991.

Stookey, Laurence Hull. *Baptism: Christ's Act in the Church.* Nashville: Abingdon Press, 1982.

Stookey, Laurence Hull. *Eucharist: Christ's Feast with the Church.* Nashville: Abingdon Press, 1993.

The United Methodist Hymnal: Book of United Methodist Worship, Nashville: The United Methodist Publishing House, 1989.

Vorgrimler, Herbert. *Sacramental Theology.* Collegeville: The Liturgical Press, 1992.

Wainwright, Geoffrey. *Eucharist and Eschatology.* New York: Oxford University Press, 1981.

Wall, W. *History of Infant Baptism, 2 Vols.* London: Adam Clark Publishing Company, 1900.

Wesley, John. *The Bicentennial Edition of the Works of John Wesley.* Gen. Eds. Frank Baker and Richard P. Heitzenrater. Nashville: Abingdon Press, 1976— .

Wesley, John and Charles. *Hymns on the Lord's Supper.* Madison, NJ: The Charles Wesley Society, 1995.

Wesley, John. *Letters.* Ed. Frank Baker. Vols. 25-26 of *The Bicentennial Edition of the Works of John Wesley.* Nashville: Abingdon Press, 1976– .

Wesley, John. *Sermons.* Ed. Albert C. Outler. Vols. 1-4 of *The Bicentennial Edition of the Works of John Wesley.* Nashville: Abingdon Press, 1976– .

Wesley, John. *The Works of John Wesley.* Ed. Thomas Jackson. 14 vols., CD-ROM edition. Franklin, TN: Providence House, 1994.

White, James F. *Sacraments As God's Self Giving.* Nashville: Abingdon Press, 1983.

Zwingli, Ulrich. *Werk,* in *Corpus Reformatorum. Vol. VIII.* Leipzig: M. Heinsius, 1834.